Your Health in Your Hands

Editors:
Medical
Dr Clemency Mitchell, MB, ChB, MRCGP
Dr Kevin Shelbourn, BMedSci, BMBS, MRCGP, DCH, DFFP

General
Julian Hibbert

Proof reader:
Andrew Puckering

Designer:
Abigail Murphy

Principal Contributor:
Dr Clemency Mitchell, MB, ChB, MRCGP

Additional Contributors:
Professor Andrew Baildam, FRCS, MD
Dr Eileen Baildam, MB, ChB, DCH, DRCOG, MRCGP, FRCP, FRCPH
G. Martin Bell, MA, MIHE
Dr Doreen Bull, MB, BS, DTM and H
Dr Martin Clee, MD
Dr R. W. Emmerson, MB, FRCP
Kristina Hammond, MA, BSc, MCSP, SRP
Fred G. Hardinge, DrPh, RD, FADA
Dr Drusilla Hertogs, MRCP, DCH
Dr W. M. Huse, MD, FRCS, FACS
Dr G. A. Jackson, BSc, MB, ChB, MFCM
Dr D. N. Marshall, BA, PhD
Dr J. W. McFarland, MD
Richard J. B. Willis, MA, MSc (Brunel), FRSH, MRIPHH, AITV, MIHE

(Chapter 13 on Belief, by Fred G. Hardinge, is reprinted, with full permission from the copyright holder, from *Celebrations*®. Copyright © 2012 by the General Conference of Seventh-day Adventists Health Ministries Department.)

Copyright © 2017 The Stanborough Press Ltd.

Printed 2017. Reprinted 2017.

All rights reserved. No part of this publication may be reproduced in any form without prior permission from the publisher.
British Library Cataloguing in Publication Data.
A catalogue record for this book is available from the British Library.

Published by The Stanborough Press Ltd,
Alma Park, Grantham, Lincolnshire, NG31 9SL, England

ISBN 978-1-78665-015-3

Printed in Serbia.

Contents

1. There is a choice 4
2. Understanding diabetes 16
3. Looking after your heart 28
4. Stress: how it works 39
5. A new approach to eating 54
6. We are what we eat 64
7. Plant food is best 80
8. Weight management 91
9. Staying fit and flexible 101
10. Good news about cancer 110
11. Dangerous addictions 122
12. Coping with allergies 141
13. Benefits of belief 148

Index 154

1 There is a choice

Disease never comes without a cause. It is not just the result of fate or our stars (horoscope), nor is it always entirely due to factors beyond our control. Most diseases are due to the simple outworking of the laws of cause and effect; they mainly result from our violations of the laws of health. This is good news, because it means that most health problems are preventable, or at least can be postponed. Our own choices can lead to better health and longer life, or poor health and early death.

In the rich countries of the industrialised world, the 'diseases of civilisation' prevail. They are responsible for most deaths and for much of the disability and chronic ill health we experience. The World Health Organisation stated that, as of 2012, cancers, diabetes, and respiratory and cardiovascular diseases were collectively responsible for 80% of all deaths caused by non-communicable diseases (NCDs). Furthermore, it also noted that NCDs were responsible for 87% of all deaths in high-income countries, 37% of deaths in the lowest-income countries, and 68% of all deaths globally.[1] These diseases are now known to result largely from the so-called 'civilised' lifestyle – the overabundant diet, with its high proportion of refined fats, sugars and animal products; a lack of exercise; the use of socially acceptable poisons like alcohol and tobacco; and the generally high levels of stress most of us are exposed to.

In the past there used to be a very different pattern of disease. Most illnesses and deaths were due to infections. Poor or non-existent sanitation and public health services allowed these infections to spread. Poverty and poor nutrition lowered people's resistance, while limited medical understanding meant that there were few effective treatments. All these factors resulted in a high incidence of infectious disease and premature death, as they still do in much of the developing world.

The picture is now changing in the developing countries, but not always for the better. The Western diet and lifestyle are becoming more and more popular with everyone who can afford them. Sedentary work and cars are in demand; Western-style high-fat fast-food outlets are multiplying; the use of tobacco and alcohol are increasing; and with all these changes, so is the incidence of degenerative disease. As a result, the poorest countries now have the double burden of a) unconquered infectious diseases, and b) the rising incidence of degenerative illnesses.

Choosing health

The laws of health are so simple that children can easily learn and understand them, but practising them is a lot more difficult. It calls for willpower and determination, especially in the face of social and commercial pressures to conform to unhealthy customs. Adhering to these laws is the route to better health, while ignoring or flouting them, sooner or later, leads to trouble.

There is one law about which we have no choice: **the law of heredity**. We all inherit our basic constitution from our forebears. We all have certain bodily strengths and weaknesses which influence our resistance and susceptibility to disease. However good or bad this inherited constitution may be, positive health choices enable us to make the very best of what we have been given. Poor choices will have the opposite effect. On average, a person's health and longevity are 20-30% due to his genes and 70-80% due to his lifestyle.[2] It has truly been said that 'Genes load the gun; lifestyle pulls the trigger.'

'Genes load the gun; lifestyle pulls the trigger.'

The other laws of health

1. The laws of activity and rest

Our bodies are designed for action. Four hours of vigorous outdoor work each day would be ideal but, unfortunately, in the West most people have sedentary jobs that leave little time for exercise. Dr Kenneth Cooper, the 'father of aerobics', found that his volunteers were relieved of all sorts of symptoms when they followed his exercise programme. Brisk exercise is, in fact, a major factor in longevity, and in the prevention of heart attacks, strokes, cancer, arthritis and many other diseases. It is also very important to those trying to recover from these problems.

2. The laws of nutrition

There should be an adequate supply of simple, wholesome food, prepared simply and naturally, and an adequate intake of clean, pure water. The type and amount of food we eat should be age- and occupation-appropriate, and in harmony with the climate we live in. Ideally one should eat at regular intervals, with the largest meals early in the day, and no between-meal or bedtime snacks. As well as being nutritious, our food should also be appetising and enjoyable.

3. The laws of abstinence from poisons

This includes those socially acceptable poisons – alcohol, tobacco and caffeine – along with all the other varieties of recreational and mind-altering substances, and all unnecessary medications. It also includes the avoidance of poisons that are found in pollutants, such as herbicides and pesticides in food, industrial and domestic pollutants and car exhaust emissions. (Realistically speaking: no one can possibly avoid all contact with pollution, but there are many choices we can make to diminish the amount we do encounter. Each of us must decide this for ourselves.)

The laws of the mind and spirit – trust in divine power

A peaceful and cheerful frame of mind is necessary for optimum health. Those who have tried it will testify that the best way to achieve this is by submitting one's life to God's will, learning about Him and obeying Him. Trust in divine power also builds trust between people – parents and children, teachers and students, colleagues and workmates. When people trust each other, it greatly reduces the interpersonal stress that contributes to disease. One way of building trust in divine power is by studying the Creator's handiwork in the design and working of our own bodies. The complexity of the human body is astounding, and inspired King David to write, 'I will praise [the Lord]; for I am fearfully and wonderfully made' (Psalm 139:14, KJV). What better motivation could there be for maintaining health, than to keep our bodies fit for our Creator's service?

4

Fighting disease

Our bodies have truly amazing **defence systems**. When danger threatens, the emergency services of the immune system go into immediate action to ward off the invaders. We, by making right choices, can actually make a great difference to their efficiency and effectiveness.

Although in the West most deaths, disabilities and chronic ill health are due to degenerative diseases, infections still cause many minor, and some major problems. Our bodies have a very active defence system to get rid of these foreign invaders. Infections occur when microorganisms – bacteria, viruses and others – invade, and the defences are mobilised as soon as they enter the body. Because most people in the West are fairly well fed and live in reasonably hygienic surroundings, their immune systems win most of the time, and they have good medical care and powerful antibiotics to take over should they start to lose. The situation is very different where there is too little food and poor sanitation. Then these invaders win much more often.

Keeping invaders out

First-line defences – Danger threatens at each place where invading organisms can gain entry into the body, and they each have their own specific defences.

The **skin** is perhaps the most obvious line of defence. Invaders can't usually enter if it is clean and intact. The **nose** is well equipped for defence against foreign material that we breathe in. Its hairs filter out the larger particles of dust, and so on, and the slippery mucus secreted by the cells lining its walls traps germs and other tiny particles, including microorganisms, so they can be blown or sneezed out. The breathing passages in the **lungs** have ciliated surfaces. Cilia are tiny, hair-like projections that work together like brushes. They beat rhythmically, moving mucus with its trapped dust and germs up to the throat, from where it can be removed by coughing or swallowing. When viruses or bacteria take hold, extra mucus is produced in an attempt to wash them out; hence the running nose or the productive cough. Colds, flu, bronchitis and pneumonia all develop from airborne organisms that enter via the nose or throat.

The tears are an important part of the **eyes'** defence system. They contain a mildly antiseptic substance which deals with most invaders. The lids, which close involuntarily when danger threatens, also have a function of washing the tears over the eye every time they blink. Extra tears wash out any dust, dirt or other undesirable substances that get in. The **ears** are self-cleaning, and the wax they produce has antibacterial properties.

Protection against invaders in food and drink begins in the **mouth**. Our saliva is mildly antiseptic, while our **stomach** juice sorts out most organisms that get that far. Some very tough bugs may survive to cause major problems further on, such as diarrhoea, as the **bowel** does its best to flush the intruders out. The **rectum**, **vagina** and **urinary passage** also have their own specific defensive properties.

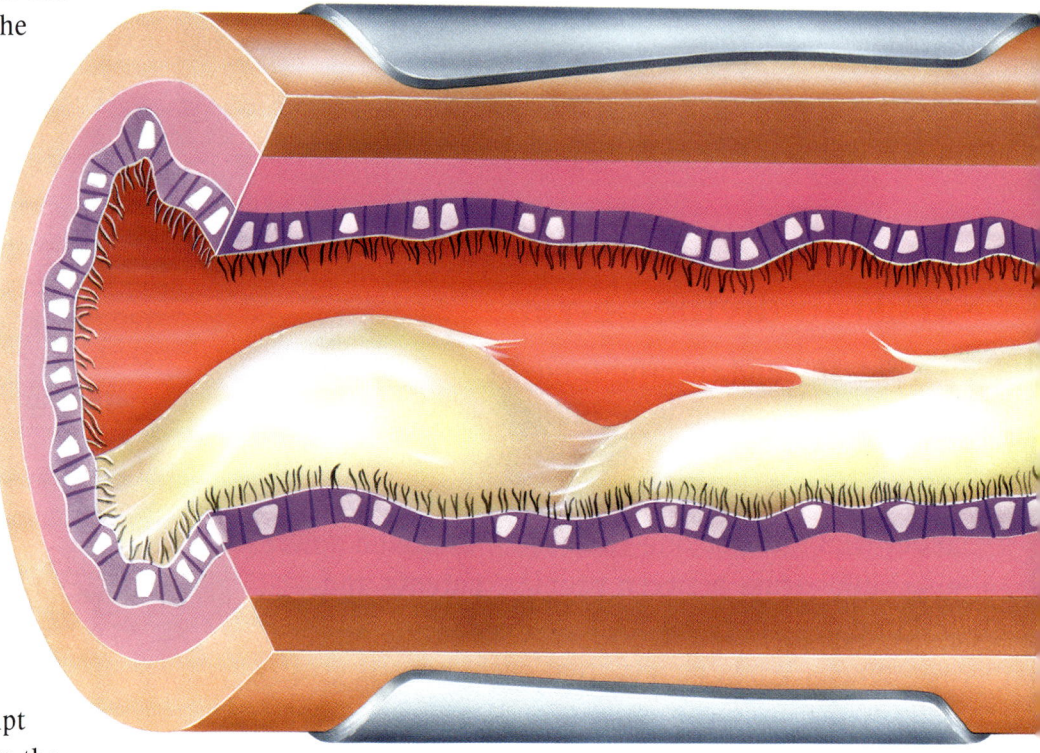

Killing invaders

Second-line defences come into action as soon as harmful microorganisms break through the first line. This is the body's major defence system, with cells stationed in every organ and tissue, and its white blood cells constantly patrolling the bloodstream and tissue fluid. It is an enormous army of cells backed up by complex support services, with huge reserves and highly efficient reinforcement production centres.

These soldiers are permanently on the alert, instantly ready to go into combat, and can call up vast reserves at short notice. They engage in various types of defensive action, including chemical warfare, and they manufacture their own special chemicals to counteract individual invading germs and their poisonous products or toxins.

The most numerous units in this army of white blood cells are usually the neutrophils. We can see their work in boils and other skin infections. Bacteria can get in through a tiny scratch on the skin and, once inside, they start to multiply rapidly. The neutros go into action straight away, each one trapping and ingesting a number of bacteria, killing and digesting them, then spitting out the remains. If there are only a few germs and lots of neutros, the neutros win and the owner of the skin isn't even aware of what has happened. This is what happens most of the time, when the immune system is working well. On the other hand, if a large number of germs get in, or if the defence is weakened for some reason, the germs may win at first. A swollen, red, painful area will develop in which the neutros are vigorously fighting the invaders. A boil will develop if enough neutros are killed. Their dead bodies will pile up in the form of pus. Fortunately, they usually win, as reinforcements are sent in, preventing the infection from spreading. The boil bursts, the dead cells are discharged, the germs have been beaten and healing takes place.

Chemical warfare!

There are also chemical warfare units. These are mainly the lymphocytes, which wait in the lymph tissues that are strategically placed throughout the body, ready for action whenever they are needed. The tonsils and adenoids are part of the lymphatic system guarding the throat, as are the lymph glands in the neck.

The lymphocytes have a number of functions, one of which is to produce **antibodies**. These are chemical weapons specifically designed to attack and neutralise foreign invaders (antigens) like germs and other enemies. This antibody-forming process takes longer than the neutros' response. It can take several weeks for them to deal with infections like chickenpox or measles but, once formed, they are designed to stay in our circulatory system for life – and, if a chickenpox or measles virus ever dares to enter again, these circulating antibodies immediately attack and inactivate it.

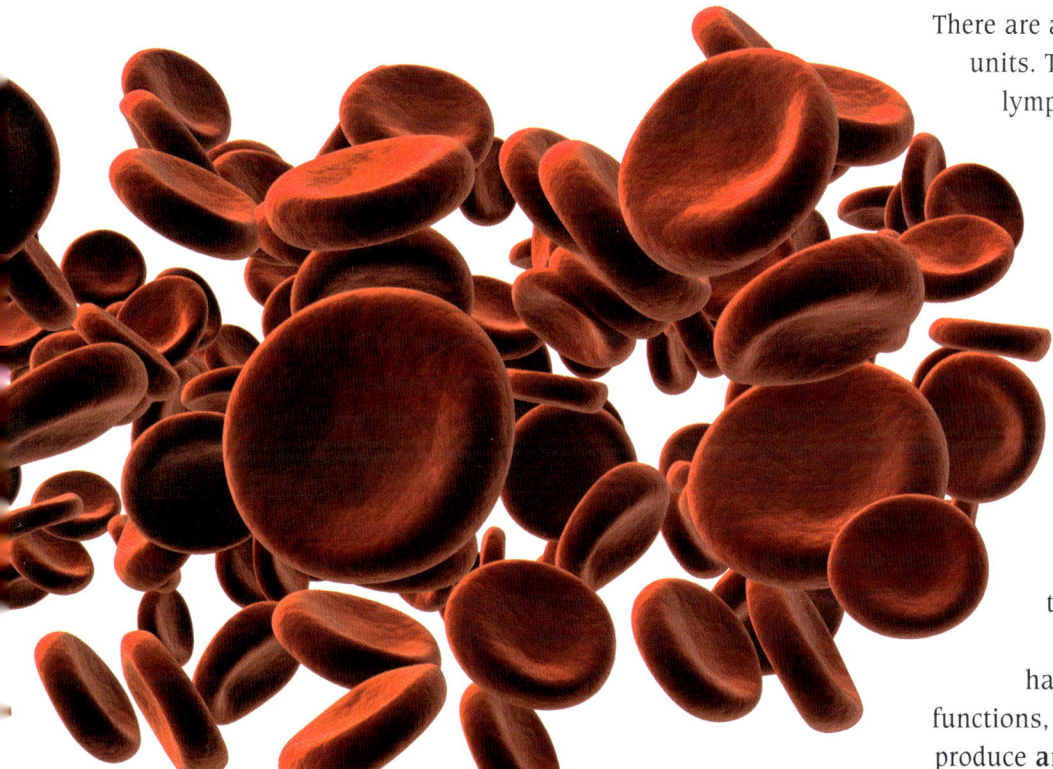

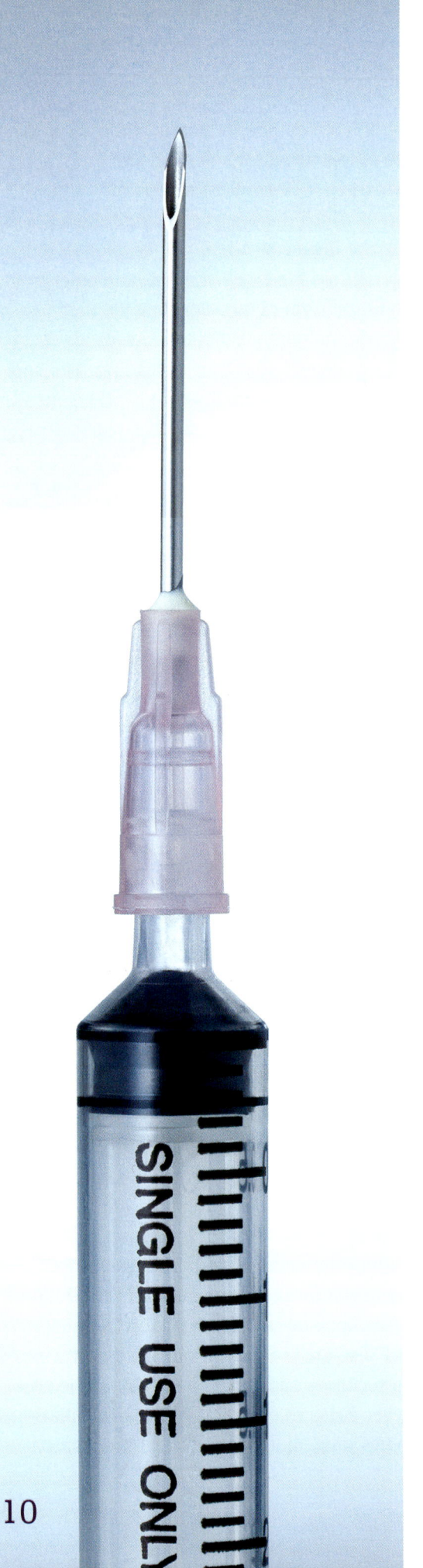

Increasing the antibody armoury

Immunisation is a method of inducing the immune system to produce antibodies that will stay in the circulation and be ready to inactivate invading organisms before they have time to produce an illness. Unfortunately they don't always produce the desired immunity, nor is it always very long-lasting: hence the need for booster doses. The idea is to prepare the body to defend itself against specific diseases, such as measles, diphtheria, tetanus, or polio, by stimulating it to produce appropriate antibodies in advance – so that, when the germs strike, the antibodies will be available at once, with no long time lag during which the disease can develop. Small doses of such organisms, which have been modified so that they are too mild to cause the disease but still have their antigens intact, are used to stimulate the lymphocytes to produce antibodies over the next few days. Then, if the real germ attacks, the disease is prevented.

Two hundred years ago Dr Edward Jenner noticed that milkmaids never got smallpox, a disease that was very common, often fatal, and usually very disfiguring. A milkmaid told him that it was because they had had cowpox, a mild illness that they caught from their cows. Dr Jenner developed the practice of vaccination, introducing cowpox organisms through scratches on the skin. Thus began the decline of smallpox, the last case of which was recorded in the 1970s.

Since then, vaccines have been developed against many other diseases, and research on others continues.

Other commonly used vaccines . . .

Diphtheria is a dangerous throat infection, which was common and frequently fatal in Europe a hundred years ago. The incidence of the disease had already greatly declined by the time the vaccine was introduced in the 1940s, and it is now largely unknown in the developed countries of the West, but still occurs in Eastern Europe and some developing countries in Africa and Asia.

Whooping cough (pertussis) is a respiratory infection mainly affecting young children. It is an unpleasant illness, often causing weeks or months of severe and distressing coughing. It can be fatal in small children, especially if they are undernourished.

Tetanus is caused by organisms which live in the digestive tracts of farm animals and survive in manure, soil and road dirt. They enter the bloodstream through wounds, especially deep penetrating ones that have been contaminated. They produce very deadly toxins that cause severe and painful muscle spasms that can be fatal if they interfere with breathing. This disease is now very rare indeed in developed countries, partly due to immunisation and partly due to better hygiene and wound care, and to improved health and nutrition in general. It is still common in those countries where there are inadequate immunisation programmes and poor hygiene, and where people are frequently in contact with animal dung. This is especially true where it is used as fuel or in building materials. Tetanus of the newborn occurs in some areas, the organisms entering through the umbilical cord stump.

Polio is a virus that enters via the digestive tract – for example, by drinking water that is polluted by sewage. It attacks the nervous system and causes muscle paralysis, which can lead to death if it paralyses the respiratory muscles. It takes its greatest toll in childhood. It is now extremely rare in countries with an effective immunisation programme, and the Word Health Organisation hopes it will soon be eliminated completely.

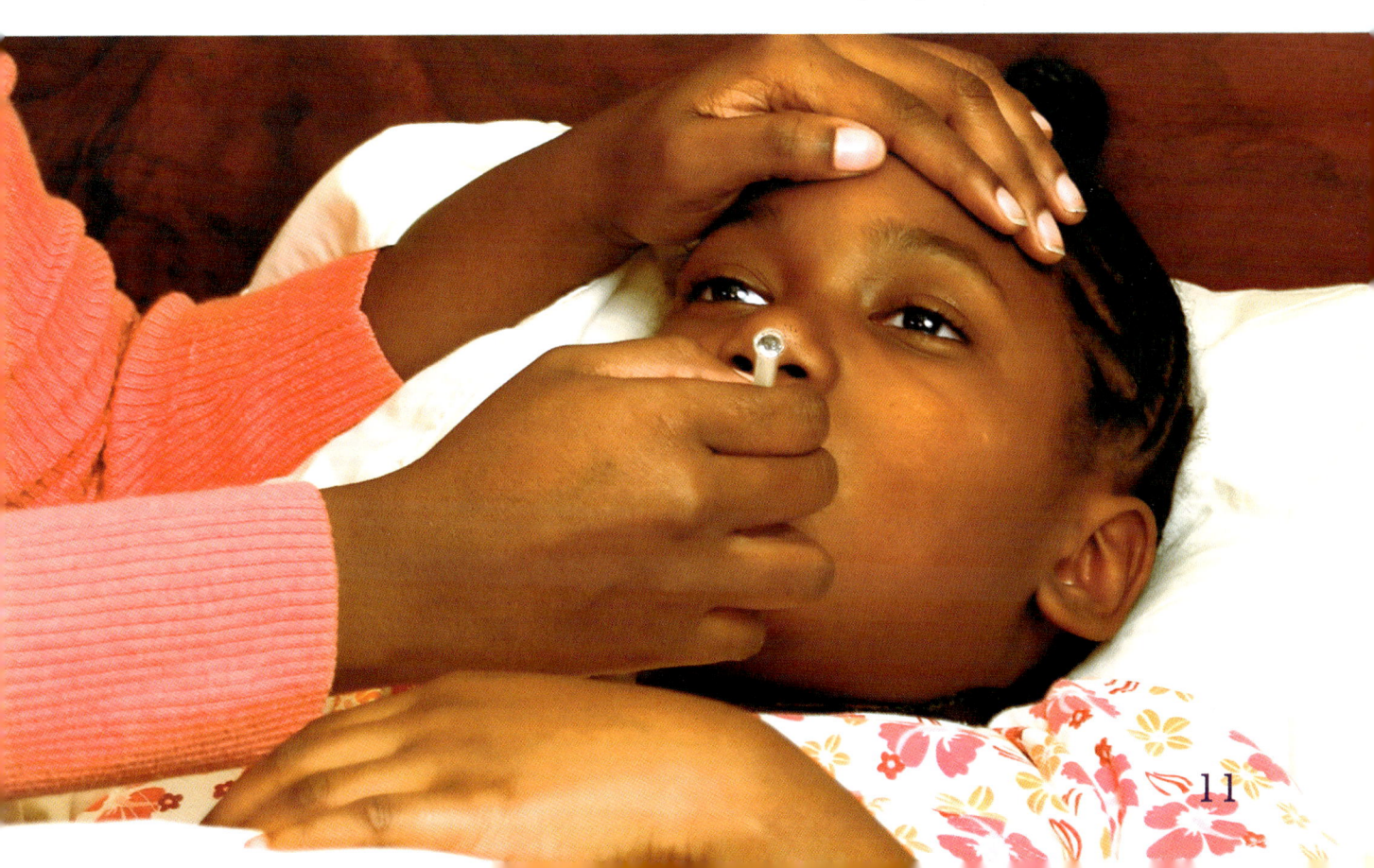

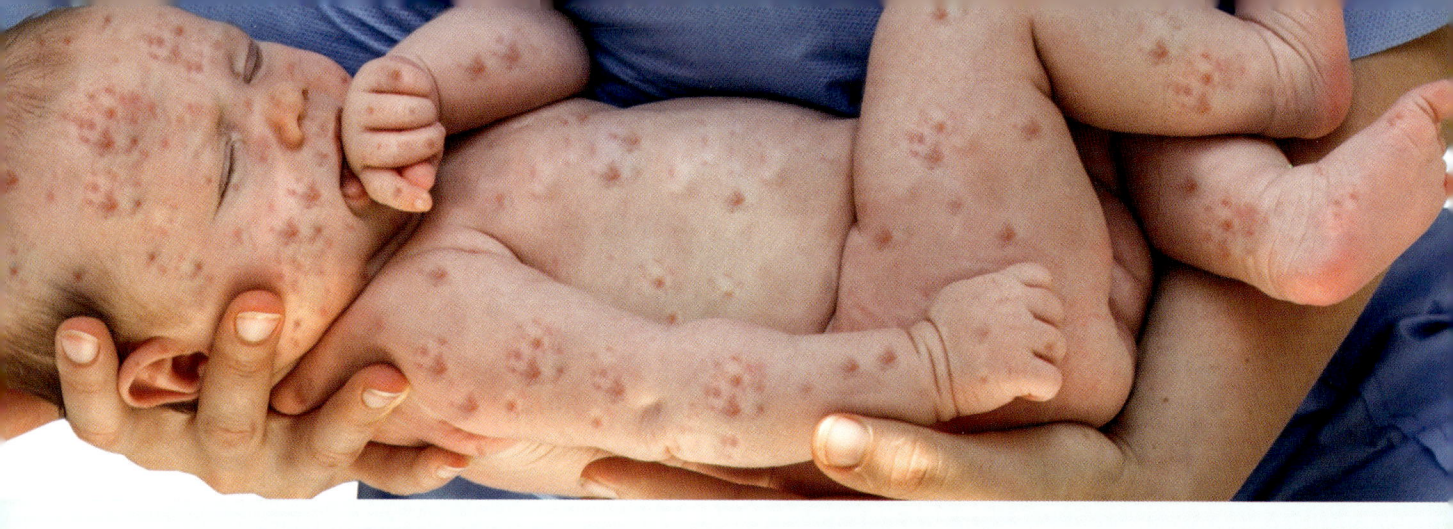

Meningitis can be caused by several different organisms. It is a dangerous disease that attacks the membranes that surround and protect the brain, and is frequently fatal. Immunisations have been developed against two of the most common and dangerous types.

MMR is a combined vaccine offering protection against measles, mumps and rubella in one shot.

Measles used to be very common. In developed countries, where children were fairly healthy and well fed, most recovered completely, but in a few rare cases there were serious complications. Some of these patients died or had severely disabling after-effects, such as deafness or blindness. In poorer countries, especially where food is inadequate and living conditions are poor, serious problems are much more common.

Mumps is usually a mild illness, but with the very occasional possibility of serious complications, such as sterility if it affects the testicles, or even death if it affects the brain. Fortunately, such cases are rare, but they are so serious that a vaccine has been developed to prevent this usually mild disease.

Rubella (German measles) is usually such a mild disease that it may not even be recognised. However, this is an illness that can have a devastating effect on the unborn child if it affects the mother during the early part of her pregnancy.

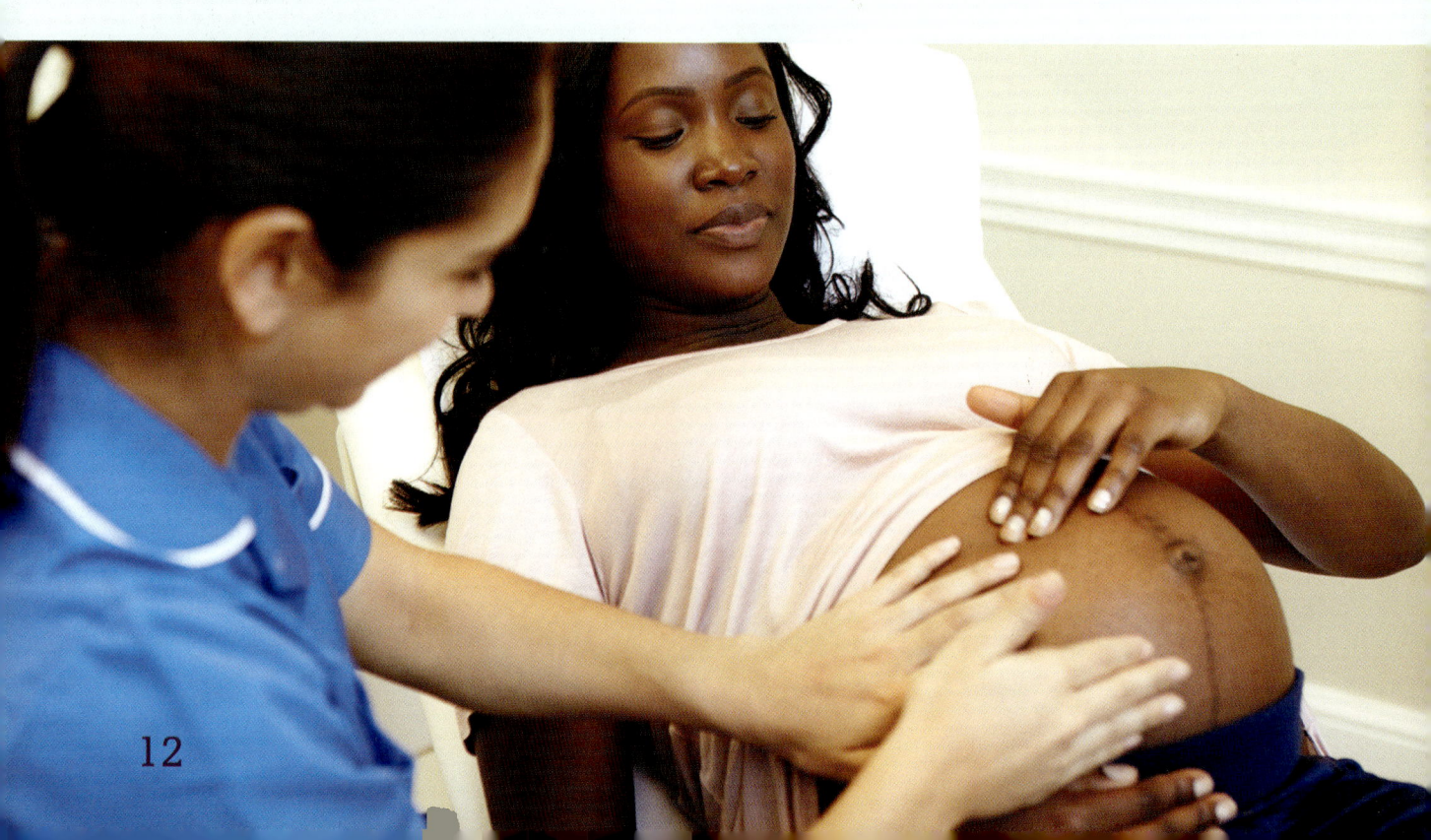

Doubts and dilemmas

As effective immunisations are developed and these infections become rarer, there is eventually a point at which the problems due to the disease are less than the problems due to the immunisation. It can also become a problem as to which immunisations should be given and when, as there is often a limit to the number of times parents can be called to bring their children to clinics for jabs, especially if they fear there may be some side effects. Already, in the UK, babies are offered immunisations against seven different organisms at the age of eight weeks, and boosters at twelve and sixteen weeks. We are assured that there is no danger in this system, and few serious side effects are ever encountered at the time, but questions have been raised as to whether this is really the best for such young immune systems.

As one group of illnesses is eliminated, another group seems to develop to take their place. In the developed countries there has been an enormous increase in childhood asthma and other allergy-related problems.[3] These are problems that involve the immune system, and some have questioned whether immunisation programmes could in some mysterious way have contributed to this. There has also been a huge increase in the diagnosis of attention deficit hyperactivity disorder (ADHD) among children in the developed countries. There may well be multiple causes for this, but some experts are wondering whether some subtle changes caused by immunisation could also contribute to this and to some cases of autism. So far the evidence of a link is considered to be inconclusive. However, it seems sensible to limit childhood immunisations to diseases that present a danger in their own particular environment, and to the ages when they are likely to encounter them. It is wise to immunise against diseases of which there is a real danger, especially those for which there is no effective treatment. Where malnutrition is a common problem, along with overcrowding, poor sanitation and hygiene, the need is even more compelling.

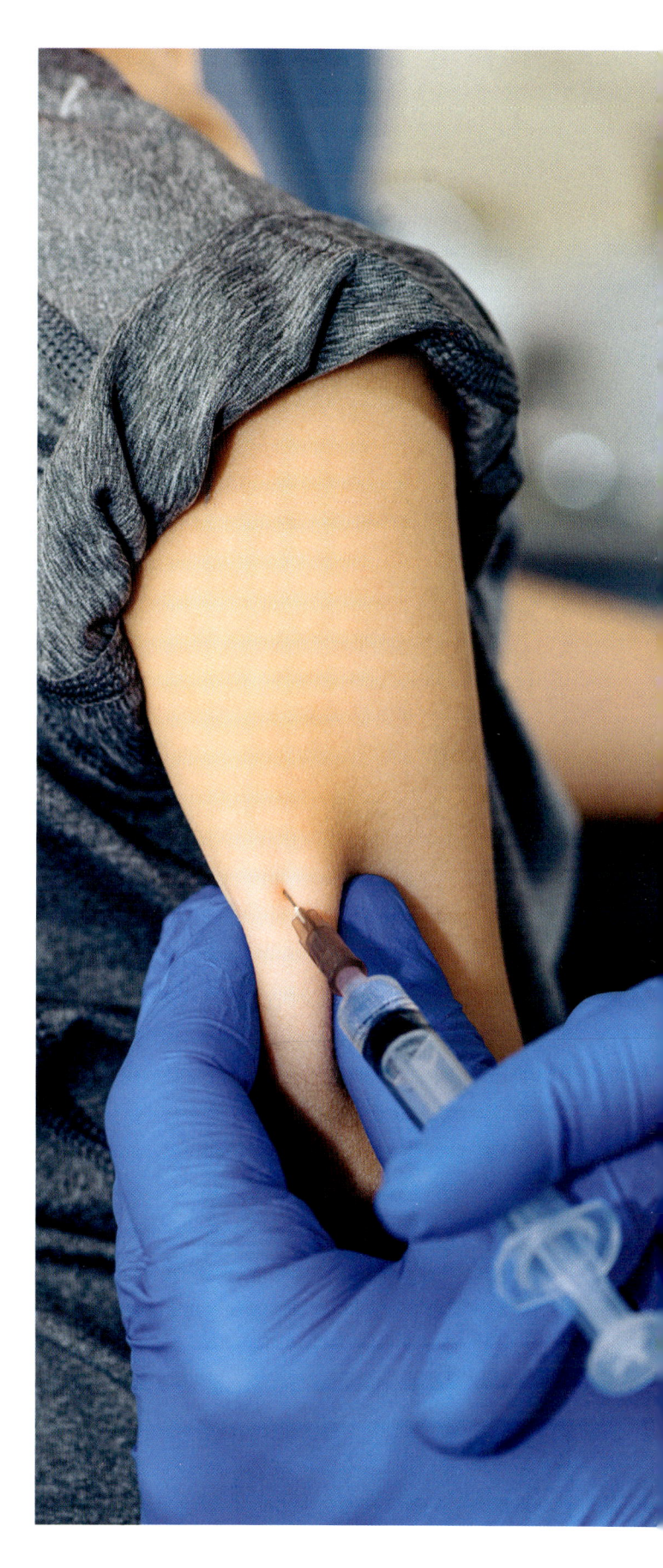

Building resistance naturally

Immunisations can obviously be lifesaving, but resistance to disease depends on much more than the presence of specific antibodies. General health and well-being are basic to our resistance to both infections and degenerative disease. There are a number of completely natural ways of boosting our defences, over which we have choices to make for ourselves and for our families.

Among its many other good effects, vigorous **exercise** increases the number of white blood cells in the circulation. It also speeds up the circulation, thereby speeding up the process of getting these defence forces to their battle stations. Regular hours for rest are very important too, because the immune system is restored while we sleep. Hormones and body cycles have inbuilt rhythms. Regular hours really are important, especially if there is a risk of illness, or if an actual illness is already present.

You can also boost your white cell count with **cold water**. Cold water on the feet sends a message of imminent danger to the immune system and calls for instant mobilisation of white cells. Dry your feet quickly and put on warm socks after the cold footbath. You will feel comfortable and your white cells will remain on the alert. A cold shower or bath has the same effect: it's a practice exercise for our immunity battalions. A cold shower may be a pleasant prospect in a warm climate, but less so during a European winter. There is good news, however, because if you take a warm bath or shower, you will get a similar effect if you simply finish off with a few seconds of cold water. Be sure to dry quickly, and within a few seconds you should feel a warm glow. The cold water will have closed down the superficial blood vessels that radiate heat after the warm bath, and you will feel warmer having had your final cold splash than you would have done had you stepped straight out of a hot tub. A word of warning: beware of chilling – too much cold when you are not used to it will leave you feeling cold, and this will have the opposite effect, of actually depressing your immune system. If you find it difficult to warm up, don't do it.

Healthy eating boosts the immune system. All the natural plant foods – the fruits, vegetables, grains, nuts and seeds – help the body's defences. There should be plenty of fruits and vegetables in our diets, some of them raw. Variety is not only the spice of life, but also an important factor in staying well. Along with their own quota of vitamins and minerals, the different plant foods each contain their own individual blend of phytochemicals, each one helping to enhance our defence systems in their own way. The refined foods, especially those high in sugar and fat, have the opposite effect.

> *'Phytochemicals'* are just 'plant chemicals', called that because they are only found in plants. They are present in minute amounts and give the plant foods their distinctive colours and flavours. They have very important immune-boosting properties and help to prevent ageing and degenerative diseases, including cancer.

Breastfed babies get passive immunity – antibodies from their mothers' blood are passed on in the milk. Breastfed babies have fewer infections of every sort, and they get a head-start in preventing future degenerative diseases.

There will be much more about the **laws of avoidance** later in the book, but it bears mentioning here that poisons, including socially acceptable ones such as nicotine and alcohol, all depress the immune system in their own specific ways.

The laws of the mind and spirit. Cheerfulness and optimism are important factors in stimulating the body's healing and defensive powers. Those who can trust in divine power for help in meeting the stresses and tensions of everyday life have a great resource. The mind has an influence on all body systems and their activity. Depression slows things down; cheerfulness stimulates. Fortunately, we are not totally at the mercy of our feelings in this matter. We can use our will to think about pleasant topics even if we are feeling terrible. Harness your willpower, and if cheerful thoughts seem impossible then just breathe a prayer of thanks for whatever positive factors you can think of. If possible, say it aloud. Read a psalm of praise, or will yourself to sing a cheering hymn or song. As you make this effort, it actually alters the chemistry of your brain. Endorphins help to lift our spirits *and* they boost the immune system too. Cheerful thoughts help to heal the body as well as the soul.

> Endorphins are substances formed in the brain by sunshine, enjoyable exercise and other pleasant experiences and thoughts.
> They stimulate the immune system to fight disease, raise the pain threshold to make discomfort more bearable, and act as natural antidepressants and tranquillisers.

[1] www.who.int/mediacentre/factsheets/fs310/en/index2.html
[2] www.scientificamerican.com/article/genetic-factors-associated-with-increased-longevity-identified/
[3] www.scientificamerican.com/article/why-are-asthma-rates-soaring/

Understanding diabetes

2

Diabetes is often in the news; in fact, in countries like the UK, it is now feared that there is such an epidemic of diabetes that it may well bankrupt the National Health Service.

What exactly is diabetes?

Diabetes is a metabolic disease that interferes with the body's management of sugar. As sugar is the body's main fuel, this is a very serious matter with very wide-ranging effects on every body system.

It's important to understand the place of sugar and insulin in how our bodies function, and here is a very simplified outline of what diabetes involves.

Sugar is our body's main fuel, the main source of energy for all our voluntary conscious activities and for all the complex and continuous metabolic (vegetative) activities that go on in our tissues without our control, to keep us alive.

All the food we eat is broken down in the digestive system into tiny components that can be absorbed into the bloodstream for transport to wherever they are needed.

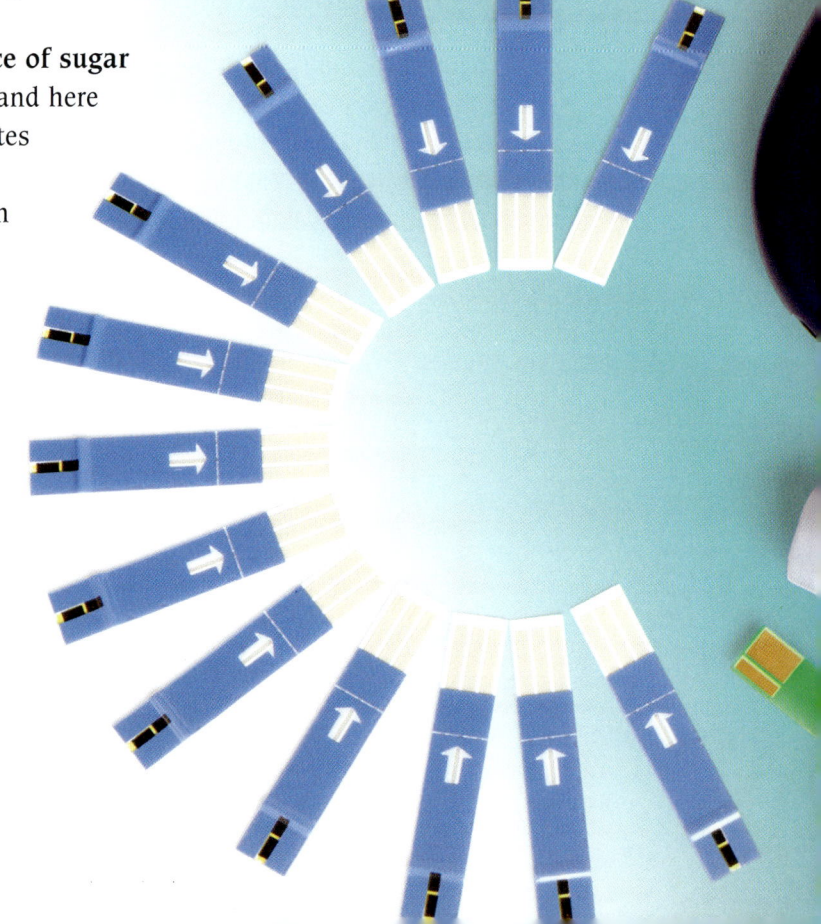

Carbohydrates – sugars and starches – are the main energy foods and these are broken down to simple sugars, mainly glucose, which enter the bloodstream and are transported throughout the body to supply every cell with the fuel it needs. Once the sugar is in the cell, it is processed with oxygen to produce energy, either for immediate use or to be stored for later. Short-term stores are found in the muscles and liver, while long-term stores are found in our fat cells.

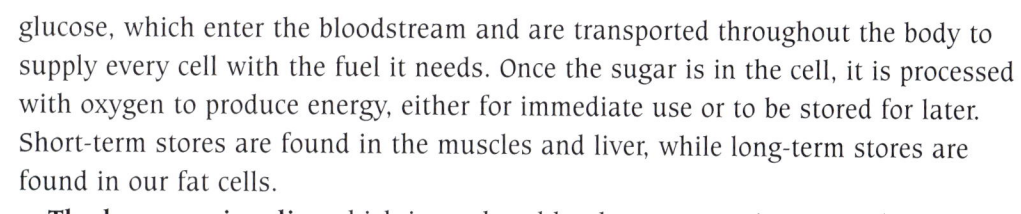

The hormone insulin, which is produced by the pancreas, is essential to this process because it's the key that opens the cells to let the sugar molecules in. The sugar can only be used inside the cells. As the blood sugar level rises after a meal, the pancreas automatically releases insulin into the bloodstream, which takes it to every cell in the body to do its vital task of letting the sugar in, and there is no way the sugar can get in without it. If there's no insulin, or if the insulin can't unlock the cells, the blood sugar level rises, and now the body has two very serious problems to cope with: no energy because the sugar can't be used, while the unused sugar builds up in the blood. The body tries desperately to reduce the sugar level and at the same time find alternative sources of energy, but unfortunately it's unable to solve these problems without causing serious damage of many kinds. This is why insulin is an absolutely key player in both type 1 diabetes, where there is no insulin, and type 2 diabetes, where the cells are so full of sugar that the insulin can't open them.

17

The two major types of diabetes

Though they have similarities, they are two different diseases.

Type 1 begins as an acute and very serious illness, most often in children or young people. Their pancreas fails to produce insulin and they need regular insulin injections to stay alive. This is also called insulin-dependent diabetes and accounts for 10% of diabetes cases.

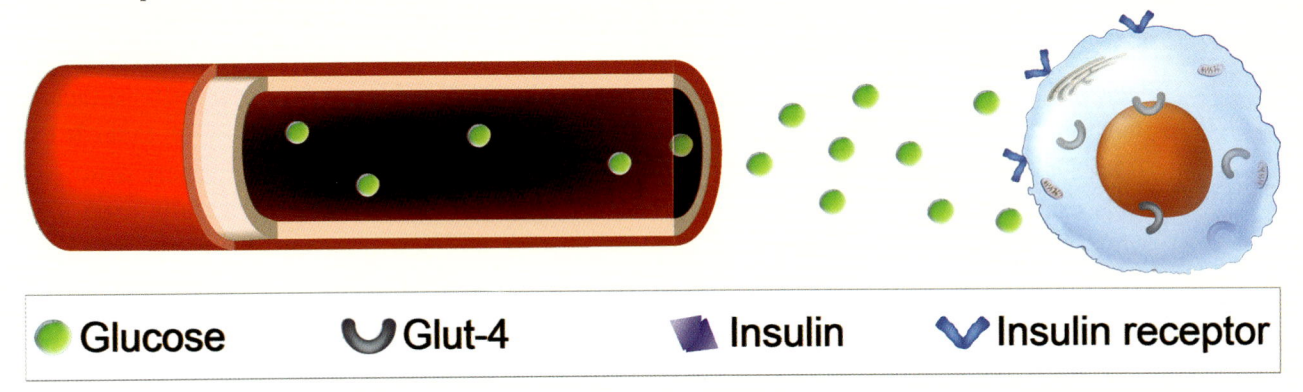

● Glucose   ∪ Glut-4   ◆ Insulin   ∨ Insulin receptor

Much more common – 90% of cases – is **type 2**, or non-insulin-dependent diabetes, which is related to diet and lifestyle and usually develops gradually over many years. The rich, high-fat, high-sugar Western diet, and the inactive Western lifestyle, are the chief culprits. This used to be known as 'maturity onset diabetes', but not any more, because over the past few decades, as calorie intake has increased and physical activity has decreased, type 2 diabetes is now occurring in teenagers and even children. As either type of diabetes progresses, serious complications develop – heart and arterial disease, kidney failure and blindness. Medical treatment can slow their development and early interventions can reduce and postpone some of the worst effects, but it does not cure. The aim is to manage the disease and reduce its effects.

Type 2 diabetes develops as the body tries to cope with excess weight and all the disruptive effects of too many calories and not enough exercise. At the cellular level, the cells are so full of sugar that they just can't take any more. They refuse to let the insulin key unlock them, so the sugar stays outside and builds up in the blood. The situation can be compared to a power station where the fuel deliveries are out of control. Far more fuel is delivered than can be used in the furnaces, all the storage areas are overflowing, so the fuel builds up wherever it can be dropped, blocking the roads, getting in everyone's way and reducing their efficiency, and eventually bringing all the work of the power station to a standstill. The solution is to increase the output

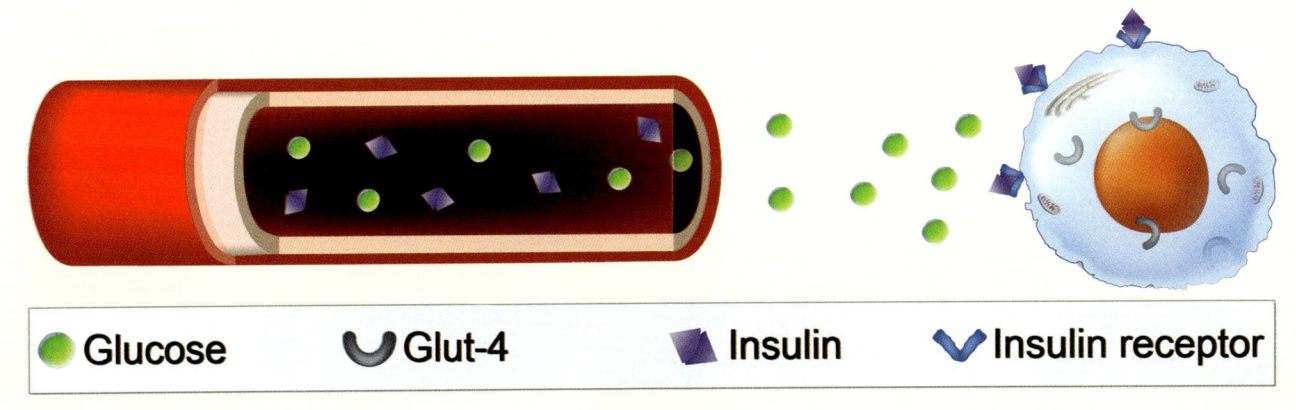

● Glucose   ∪ Glut-4   ◆ Insulin   ∨ Insulin receptor

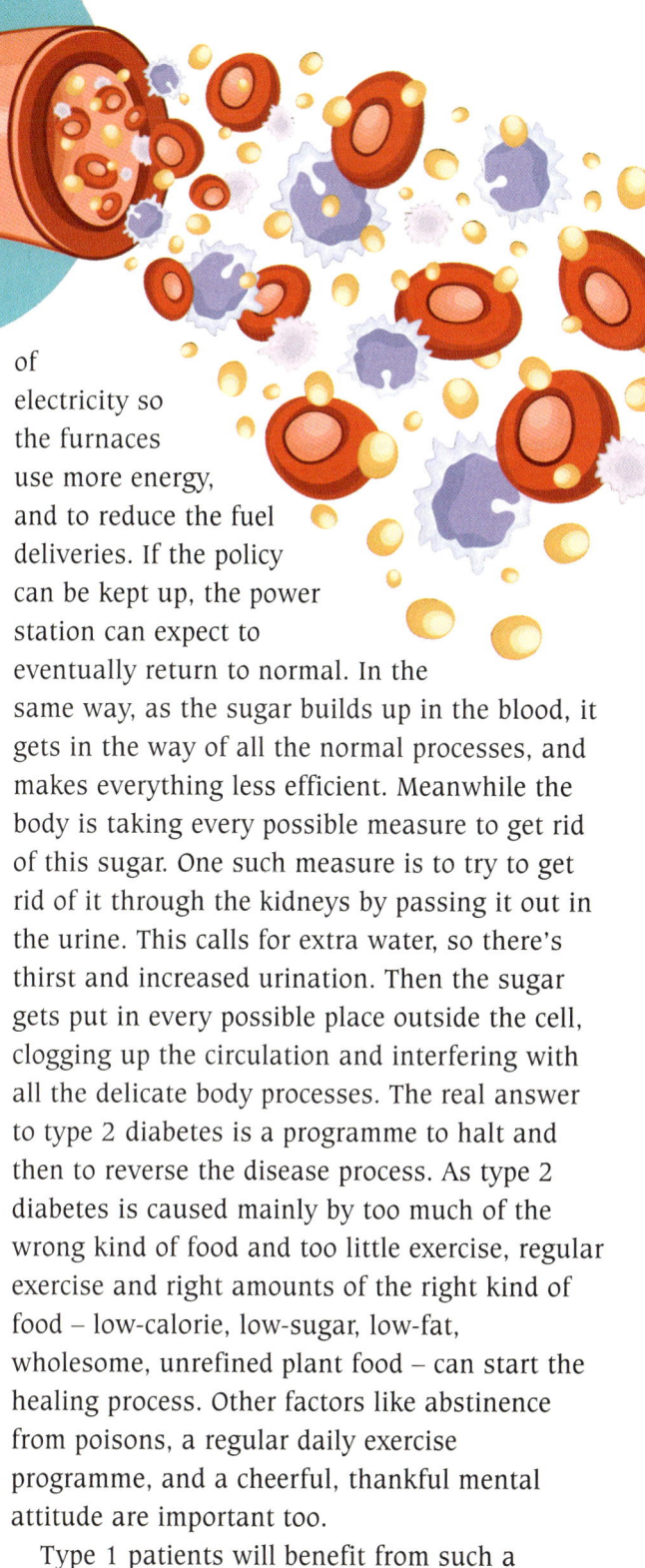

of electricity so the furnaces use more energy, and to reduce the fuel deliveries. If the policy can be kept up, the power station can expect to eventually return to normal. In the same way, as the sugar builds up in the blood, it gets in the way of all the normal processes, and makes everything less efficient. Meanwhile the body is taking every possible measure to get rid of this sugar. One such measure is to try to get rid of it through the kidneys by passing it out in the urine. This calls for extra water, so there's thirst and increased urination. Then the sugar gets put in every possible place outside the cell, clogging up the circulation and interfering with all the delicate body processes. The real answer to type 2 diabetes is a programme to halt and then to reverse the disease process. As type 2 diabetes is caused mainly by too much of the wrong kind of food and too little exercise, regular exercise and right amounts of the right kind of food – low-calorie, low-sugar, low-fat, wholesome, unrefined plant food – can start the healing process. Other factors like abstinence from poisons, a regular daily exercise programme, and a cheerful, thankful mental attitude are important too.

Type 1 patients will benefit from such a programme as well. They won't be able to restore their lost insulin production so they won't be able to stop their injections, or escape their need for medical supervision, but their diabetes will become easier to control, complications will be less severe, their general health will improve and they will be more in control of their lives.

The obesity connection

Why is type 2 diabetes so common now? It is closely related to obesity, and because there is a worldwide epidemic of obesity, the scene is set for a worldwide epidemic of type 2 diabetes. Most people with type 2 diabetes are overweight and many are obese. Most obese people are at serious risk of developing type 2 diabetes, as well as many other serious problems.

According to the WHO, worldwide obesity has nearly doubled since 1980. By 2008, 35% of adults aged 20 and over were overweight and 11% were obese. According to the UK's National Health Service (NHS) Information Centre, around 30% of children aged between two and five years old were overweight and half of those were obese. UK obesity rates are among the highest in Europe and have increased dramatically over the last few years. More than half the population are overweight and over 20% are obese.

On average obesity decreases life expectancy by nearly 10 years. It greatly increases the risk of developing type 2 diabetes as well as high blood pressure, heart attacks, strokes, and numerous other life-shortening conditions.

Obesity develops when there is an ongoing imbalance between energy intake (food) and energy output (exercise). The World Health Organisation identified that reduction of physical activity and increased intake of energy-dense, nutrient-poor food (sugar and fat-rich 'junk foods') have led to the increase in weight with its subsequent increase in type 2 diabetes incidence. It's a worldwide problem, with some of the most affected areas being North America, the United Kingdom, Eastern Europe, the Middle East, Pacific Islands, Australasia and China, where obesity has risen threefold since 1980. Although these developed areas have the highest incidence, even in the poorest countries there are people living sedentary and overfed lifestyles.

The economic burden is high everywhere. In the UK, one of the rich developed countries, 6% of the population are diagnosed as diabetic and their care accounts for 10% of the health service budget. But because it develops slowly, and may not be diagnosed for years, there may be many more cases. In the poor countries, already burdened with infectious diseases, malnutrition and poor medical services, the extra burden of the degenerative diseases makes their situation dire.

Type 1 diabetes is an acute, life-threatening illness that affects young people, including children, and is rare over 40. It can begin suddenly as an acute medical emergency, especially in children, though occasionally it may develop over a couple of weeks. It is an auto-immune disease that destroys the insulin-producing cells of the pancreas. The cause is unknown and the treatment is insulin replacement. Without insulin replacement it is fatal within weeks or months.

> Obesity develops when there is an ongoing imbalance between energy intake (food) and energy output (exercise).

Obesity definition

Body mass index (BMI) is a simple index of weight-for-height measurements that is commonly used to classify overweight and obesity in adults. It is defined as a person's weight in kilograms divided by the square of his height in metres (kg/m^2). The WHO definition is: a BMI greater than or equal to 25 is overweight; over 30 is obese. A simpler, less accurate concept of obesity is 20% above recommended body weight. With either of these calculations, waist circumference is even more important than the weight itself. This is because excess abdominal fat surrounding the internal organs is a more important predictor of trouble than fat stored elsewhere.

---

fat stores were depleted as the body attempted to get energy from protein and fat. By-products of this abnormal process would build up in the bloodstream and lead to confusion, and eventually coma and death.

Fortunately this situation is seldom seen since the discovery of insulin in the early 1920s – one of the most dramatic medical breakthroughs of all time. Insulin injections bring immediate relief and if continued regularly, with good medical care, they allow diabetics to live a

With treatment and good medical care, life can be almost normal, though life expectancy is reduced.

This disease has been known since the days of ancient Greece, where it was known as a fatal disease characterised by severe thirst, drinking large amounts and passing large amounts of urine (polyurea), weakness and weight loss. It was only in the late nineteenth century that it began to be understood, and only in the 1920s that insulin was discovered, isolated, and could be used to treat patients. The name 'diabetes' comes from classical Greek, meaning 'passing through', from the increased thirst resulting in increased urine, and 'mellitus', meaning sweet, because some noted that the urine tasted sweet.

A typical case would be that of a young person who, after an acute fever, suddenly became very seriously ill. The patient would be very thirsty and need to drink vast amounts, resulting in polyurea as the kidneys tried to get rid of the excess sugar. As their cells could no longer process sugar to produce energy, they became very weak, and as the body desperately tried to find other sources of energy the whole metabolism was disrupted. Muscles wasted and nearly normal life for many years. As diabetes was no longer fatal, it was gradually observed that there was more to diabetes and high blood sugar than simply a lack of insulin. There were still problems with body chemistry, particularly with fat metabolism, that brought greater risk of life-shortening problems: heart attacks, strokes and kidney failure, reducing life expectancy by at least twenty years, and increasing the chance of severe disabilities, including blindness.

Over the years there have been many advances. Blood sugar levels can be measured much more accurately and easily and thereby brought under much better control, so people with type 1 diabetes can now live much longer and healthier lives. Management is much easier now than for the first survivors. Instead of time-consuming urine checks to monitor blood sugar levels, there are quick and easy blood sugar tests that are much more accurate. Injections used to be a time-consuming exercise, with glass syringes and needles to be sterilised. Now all the equipment is very user-friendly and far more efficient and accurate. One of the wonders of genetic engineering is that human insulin can now be produced by specially programmed bacteria and insulin need no longer be produced from animal pancreases. With good supervision, complications are noted earlier, prompt action can be taken, and healthy, disability-free life expectancy has greatly increased.

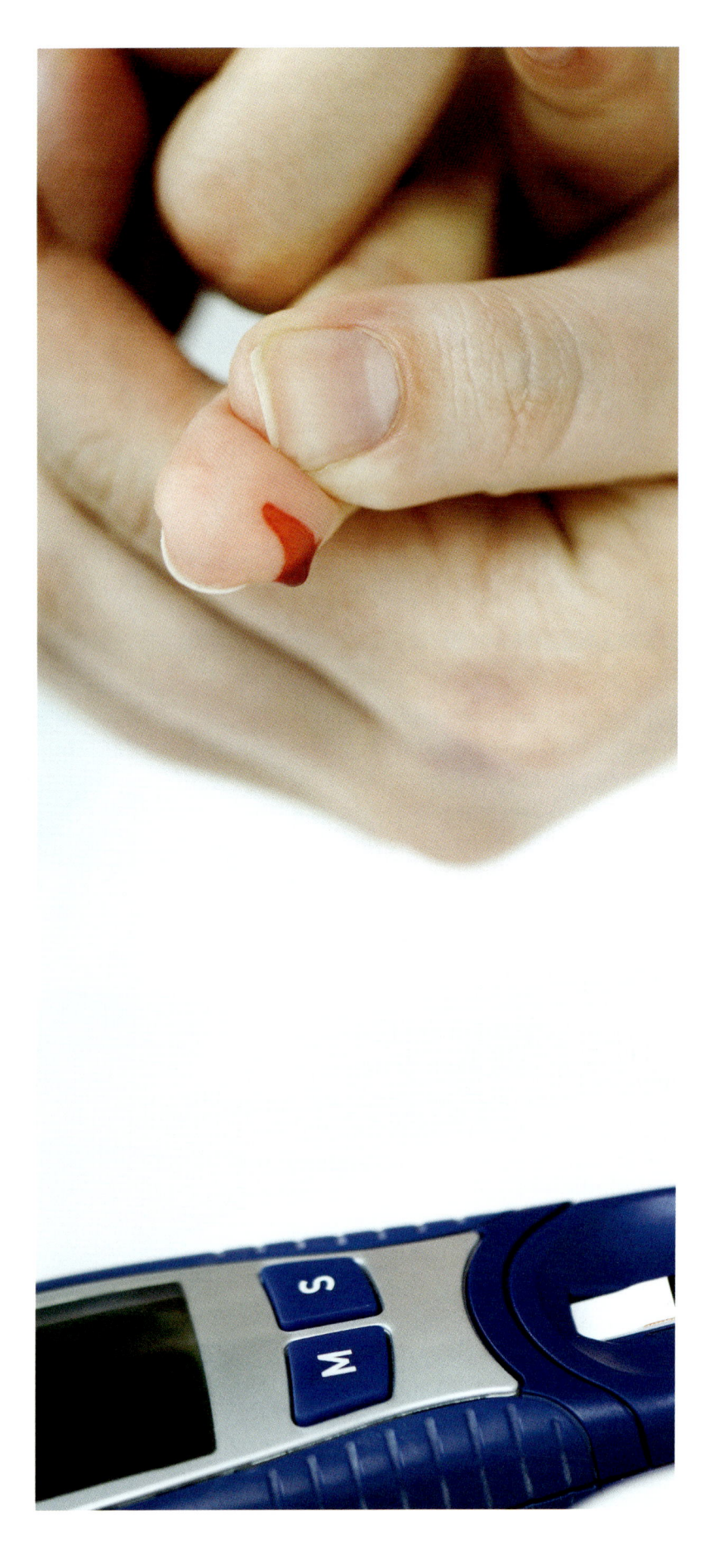

The story of Banting and Best

When scientists first began to take a serious interest in diabetes, towards the end of the nineteenth century, it had been recognised as an incurable and rapidly fatal disease for over 3,000 years. Very little was known about what caused it and even less about how to cure it. Some decades before, a medical student named Langherhans had discovered that there are islands of different sorts of cells in the pancreas. The cell groups were named the Islets of Langerhans, but their significance was quite unknown. In 1889 scientists discovered that dogs developed diabetes-like symptoms and soon died if their pancreases were removed. In 1910 another scientist suggested the dogs had died because they lacked a single chemical from the islet cells of the pancreas. He didn't know what it was, but he named it anyway – insulin, after the island cells discovered fifty years before.

In 1921 a young surgeon, Frederick Banting, was lecturer at the University of Toronto Physiology Department. He was already a remarkable man. An army surgeon in the Great War, he had been awarded the Military Cross for his bravery and altruism in continuing to treat wounded soldiers for many hours after he himself had been wounded. He came across an article about diabetes that aroused his interest. McLeod, the professor in charge of his department, was also interested and, as he was about to leave for the summer, assigned him a lab to work in, a medical student assistant (Charles Best) and ten laboratory dogs. That summer was the start of perhaps the most exciting in any medical research establishment anywhere. The first breakthrough was to reverse diabetes in a dog whose pancreas had been removed, by injecting it with an extract of ground-up pancreatic island cells. James Collip, an enthusiastic young biochemist, joined their team to isolate the insulin from the cell extract. Within a month of isolating the insulin he had a form that was suitable for injection into humans and Banting and Best used it to treat a very sick 14-year-old boy, who weighed less than 30 kg and was very close to death. The injection was an immediate success, and they successfully treated 6 more patients. That was in 1922, and by the next year insulin was being mass-produced and 25,000 people were being treated in the US and Canada, and very soon after that the treatment was available worldwide. Diabetes was no longer a fatal disease preceded by rapidly failing health.

In 1923 Banting and McLeod jointly received the Nobel Prize. Banting shared his with his student assistant Best, and McLeod shared his with Collip, the biochemist who purified the insulin. They shared the patent for the discovery of insulin with the University of Toronto and took no profit for themselves. Banting, Best and Collip all went on to have distinguished careers in medical research.

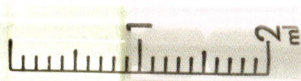

Type 2 diabetes was much less common in 1922 and was only recognised as a separate disease in the 1930s, when Sir Harold Himsworth published a paper distinguishing insulin-dependent and insulin-resistant diabetes. Although both kinds of diabetes are disorders of sugar metabolism where sugar builds up in the blood because it can't enter the cells, the reasons for this are completely different. Type 2 diabetes is a chronic disease, which was seen as one of the 'diseases of civilisation' associated with an inactive lifestyle, abundant food and middle-age obesity: a problem mainly for overweight over-40s in the rich countries of the West. But as Western diet and lifestyle have become more common elsewhere, so has type 2 diabetes. Its incidence has vastly increased over the last few decades and it's becoming a problem in nearly all countries where people aspire to the Western lifestyle with its refined-food diet full of sugar, fat and animal protein, and its lack of exercise. It is now the seventh-commonest cause of death worldwide.

And it's not only a disease of prosperity; changes in the food industry in many parts of the world have brought about situations where the refined, processed, high-fat and sugary food is cheaper and much easier to access than healthy food.

As type 2 diabetes is a chronic disease that develops slowly, it might not be diagnosed for years, and it might be discovered by chance at a routine medical, or during the treatment of some other illness. The typical patient is over 40, obese and physically inactive, but as obesity becomes more widespread younger people, even teenagers and children, are at risk. There is a genetic component and also an ethnic one: in the UK people from a South Asian background are most at risk and are likely to develop the disease 10 or more years earlier than those with an African or Afro-Caribbean background. In the USA it's the Hispanic people who have the highest risk, followed by the African Americans. However, wherever obesity is common, so is type 2 diabetes, whatever the ethnic background.

What are the complications of diabetes? The high blood sugar levels have widespread damaging effects, particularly on the circulation. In arteries it combines with cholesterol to form plaques, which narrow the vessels and contribute to coronary artery disease and stroke. In the kidneys it affects the small blood vessels blocking the supply of oxygen to the tissues, causing gradual kidney failure. Diabetes is the commonest cause of kidney failure and reason for kidney transplant. In the eye it damages the tiny vessels in the retina, leading eventually to blindness. Sugar molecules lodge in the lens and lead to cataracts, which, but for high-tech surgery, would also cause blindness. In the feet it also blocks blood vessels, reducing the circulation to the extremities, actually killing the tissues and risking gangrene, necessitating amputations of toes, feet, or even legs. At the same time it causes damage to peripheral nerves, causing a very painful and difficult-to-treat peripheral neuropathy.

Excess sugar in the skin slows the healing of wounds and promotes yeast infections like thrush in warm, moist areas where skin folds touch, and boils and other septic infections in other areas.

This is a very gloomy list of very common life-changing and life-shortening complications that threaten diabetes patients if there is no good medical care. Good medical care can prevent or postpone many of these developments, and others can be treated and modified. Better still, if good care is coupled with lifestyle change, many of the processes can be reversed.

Good medical care involves regular supervision where blood pressure, weight, kidney function, blood sugar and cholesterol levels are measured. The eyes are examined for retinal damage, and the feet for circulation and nerve function. Any abnormalities can then be picked up early and referred to the appropriate specialists for further action. Such regular care, aimed at keeping blood sugar levels consistently low, has done much to reduce or postpone the development of complications and to lengthen life. Where appropriate, medication can be prescribed. These are essential, but in no way do they actually cure the underlying problems.

The truly wonderful news is that, if lifestyle

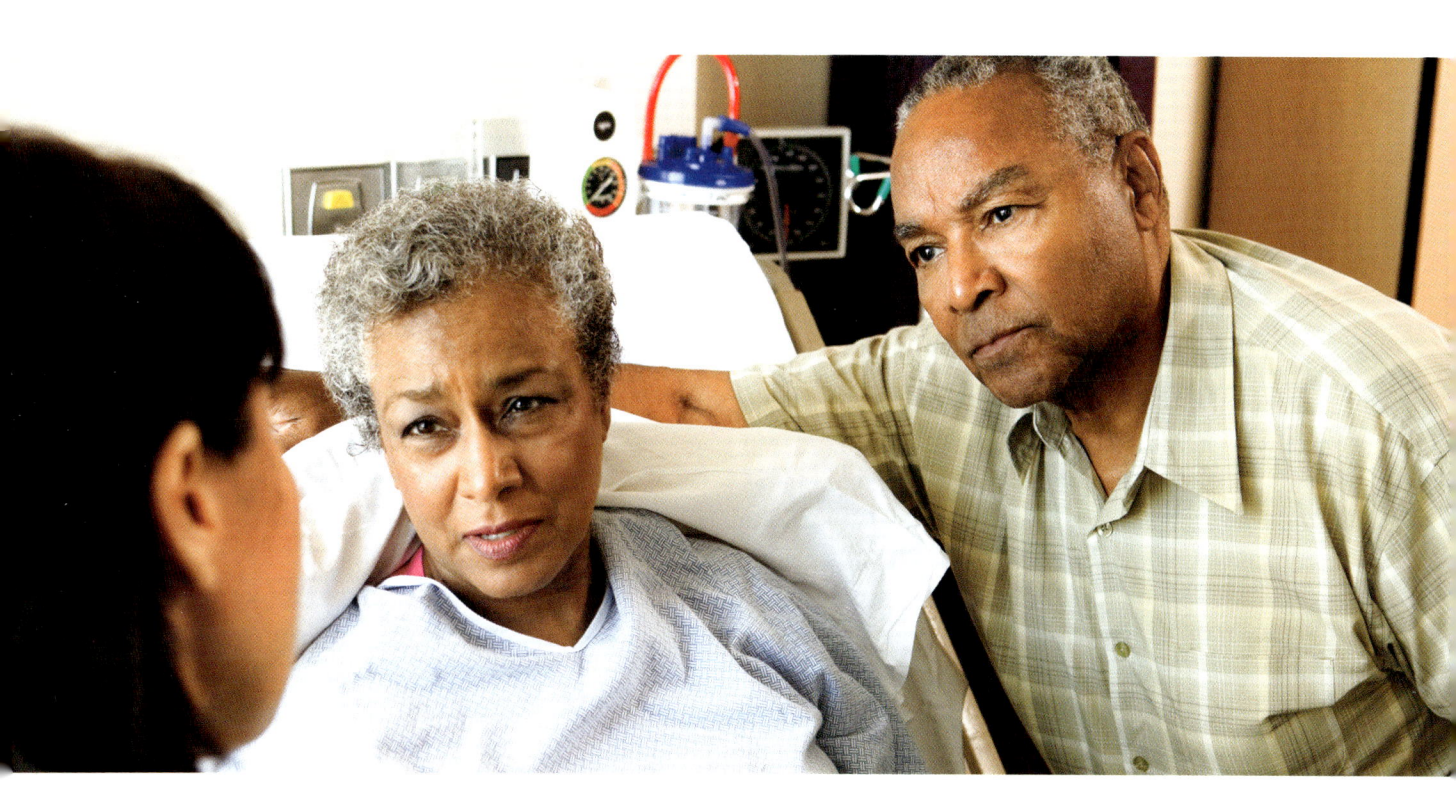

changes are made early on, the diabetic disease process can be reversed. Even in advanced cases the situation can be improved and the disease slowed down.

Medication can never be as successful as lifestyle change, because it doesn't get to the root of the problem but concentrates on symptoms. If the problem is overstuffed cells, concentration on lowering the blood sugar with medicines simply allows the disease process to continue. Lifestyle change aims at stopping or reversing the process.

In type 2 diabetes the sugar can't get in because the cells are already overloaded with sugar and refuse to accept any more – they have become insulin resistant. There are two solutions to this problem – the first is to empty the cells so they can take more sugar in: exercise uses up the sugar already in the cells, and lower-calorie food reduces the level of sugar in the blood. The second is the conventional medical treatment of medication to lower the blood sugar. This is a complex and lifelong undertaking, which aims to monitor and control the disease process, keeping the blood sugar within safe limits and postponing complications. At the same time patients are encouraged to reduce their weight, become more active and choose a lower-calorie diet, and on this regime some do lose weight and keep the blood sugar level low enough to avoid the need for medication. However, many doctors have little success in persuading their patients to make the lifestyle changes and turn to medication.

Changing the lifestyle that caused the trouble in the first place is the right way to go, getting to the root of the problem, and in the long term this will be the most satisfactory.

A lifestyle programme to help all people with diabetes:

Prevention is better than cure. Type 2 diabetes is one of the most preventable conditions. As it's known to be a lifestyle-related disease, particularly related to obesity, the healthy lifestyle habits that prevent or control obesity are the ones that can prevent type 2 diabetes and even start to reverse the disease process.

Although, as yet, it's not known how to prevent type 1 diabetes, the same healthy lifestyle features can help to prevent or at least postpone many of the complications. They won't be able to restore the lost insulin production, so patients won't be able to stop their injections, or escape all medical supervision, but their diabetes will become easier to control, complications will be less severe, their general health will improve and they will be more in control of their lives.

For many this will call for a complete change of lifestyle; for others, it will mean some simple dietary changes and increased exercise to normalise their weight.

Right eating: the low-calorie, low-sugar, low-fat, whole, unrefined plant food diet is the answer. To reverse the disease process it is necessary to eat only as many calories as the body requires and to ensure that those calories come from 100%-nutritious food that contains all the micronutrients needed for restoring and healing the damaged tissues. This is the diet based on unrefined starches (wholemeal bread and other unrefined cereal products), vegetables, fruits, nuts and seeds (beans, lentils and so on). The diet to control weight and to lower blood sugar is the same diet for lowering blood pressure and blood cholesterol and reversing heart disease. Meal timing is important too, as it is best to eat at regular times and with the main meals at the times when energy is needed for the day's activities. This usually means a big breakfast and lunch and a light evening meal.

Exercise: the right amount of exercise for most can be as simple as a half-hour brisk walk twice a day, or less.

Other lifestyle factors like abstinence from poisons are important. Tobacco is particularly undesirable because it causes arteries to constrict. When the arteries are already damaged this can literally make all the difference between life and death, and alcohol, being a source of many empty calories, should be avoided or at least very strictly limited. A regular daily programme and a cheerful, thankful mental attitude are very important too.

What about those already on medication? Even those with advanced disease can benefit from lifestyle changes, but should discuss their plans with their medical advisers and should not reduce their medication without discussing it with them.

A social and cultural problem with strong economic connections. In many places the cheapest food is high-fat, high-sugar junk food. Vast numbers of people have left their rural environments to look for a better life in cities, only to find a very bad life where health is concerned. Inadequate housing means inadequate cooking facilities, and low incomes demand long hours of work, leaving little time to shop or cook, or even look for healthy food.

In many parts of the world parents are too anxious to let their children out to play and are too busy to go out with them. Screen time in front of computers or TVs seems a safer option.

Two-income families have many stresses – driving everywhere to hold down the jobs and deliver the children to places that can be quite far apart. In these sorts of situations one has to do the best one can, to make careful plans to make the most of what is there, making changes gradually where possible.

When to seek medical help

Type 1 diabetes often presents as an acute medical emergency, especially in a child. It develops over a few weeks at most. Symptoms soon become very obvious (weakness, excessive thirst and urination, and weight loss), and often the patient is so ill that you would seek medical help anyway, whatever the symptoms. So get help at once!

Type 2 diabetes is quite the opposite. The symptoms are often so mild and vague that it's usually diagnosed on a routine blood test, or in the course of another health problem. Suspicious symptoms, especially in older overweight and obese people, include thirst and excessive urination; skin infections in genital areas and skin folds; and general weakness and feeling unwell. See your doctor and ask for a blood test.

3 Looking after your heart

Cardiovascular disease is the world's number-one killer. According to the World Health Organisation it claimed 17.5 million lives in 2012 – that is 3 in every 10 deaths.[1] In the rich countries of the West, diseases of the heart and circulation cause more than fifty per cent of all deaths. The poorer countries are suffering from these diseases more and more, and they are now the leading cause of all deaths worldwide.

In America and Western Europe, although heart disease is still the number-one killer, the incidence has fallen a little in the last few decades, probably mainly due to people smoking less. The incidence varies from country to country and between different parts of the same country. In the UK it's quite a lot higher in the north-west than in the south-east. As the incidence has been falling in America and Western Europe, it has risen in Eastern Europe.[2]

The Western lifestyle kills! As far as the developing world is concerned, the more Westernised the diet and lifestyle become, the higher the incidence of cardiovascular disease. This is a very serious problem to those developing countries that have not yet overcome the problems of infectious disease. They now have a double burden: the diseases of wealth in one part of the population, and the diseases of poverty in the rest.

Heredity or lifestyle?

Many different factors contribute to the incidence of cardiovascular disease. Heredity is important, but lifestyle is even more important. Those with a family history of heart attacks, strokes and other diseases of the heart and circulation are more at risk. The risk increases with age, and is higher in males, though after the menopause women start to catch up. The rest of the risks concern lifestyle factors, which can be changed and about which most people can make choices. Healthy lifestyle choices ensure that one makes the most of the life one has and postpones the inherited problems for as long as possible. 'Genes load the gun, lifestyle pulls the trigger.'

Risk factors

There are four very important and well-known medical risk factors, which were first widely demonstrated by the famous study in the small American town of Framingham that was started in 1949, and is still going on. By the late 1970s it became clear that the people of that town who had these conditions were at a much higher risk of coronary heart disease than those who did not. These conditions associated with heart disease are high blood cholesterol, high blood pressure, obesity and diabetes. They are all very much affected by lifestyle factors, especially diet. Any one of them alone will increase the risk, and the more of them there are present, the higher the risk.

Smoking alone actually raises the risk of cardiovascular disease more than any other factor, and compounds the risk when any of the other factors are present. Physical inactivity and stress are also important negative factors. These findings suggested that factors that lower blood cholesterol, blood pressure, blood sugar and weight would reduce the incidence of heart disease. The World Health Organisation Cardiovascular Disease Prevention Team state that 50% of cardiovascular disease could easily be prevented if people could be persuaded to adopt healthier lifestyles. Those working in lifestyle medicine are convinced that an optimal programme will prevent 90% of this disease. Such a programme is one that includes healthy eating, vigorous exercise, freedom from poisons, and freedom from harmful stress.

Reversing the risks

Not only can cardiovascular disease be prevented: it can be *reversed*. Nathan Pritikin, who was not a medical man but an engineer, set up a programme in the 1970s in Southern California, which worked wonders in relieving the symptoms of cardiovascular disease. Similar methods are used at the Weimar Institute, also in California, and a number of other places, with outstanding results. But it was only when Dean Ornish, at the University of Sacramento in the early 1990s, published a paper demonstrating that coronary artery blockages actually decreased on his programme, that the medical profession began to accept that the disease could be reversed. His programme included a very low-fat, very low-cholesterol diet, regular exercise and stress control. His patients had angiograms (special imaging techniques that measure the diameter of the coronary arteries) at the beginning and end of the programme. He also had a control group of patients with similar problems, but who were not on the programme. The angiograms showed that over 80% of those on the programme had regression of their arterial disease: that means that their arteries were less blocked. Over 80% of the control group's arteries were *more* blocked at the end of the year-long research programme.

How the heart works

The heart is quite simply a pump, with extraordinary powers of self-servicing and self-repairing. It is built from a unique type of muscle fibre with a built-in electrical conducting system to co-ordinate its action. It beats around seventy times a minute, totalling 100,000 beats a day; never stopping as long as life lasts, and only resting in the fraction of a second between beats. If it should stop for more than a few seconds we would lose consciousness, and if it were not started within a few minutes, irreversible brain damage would occur, and soon after that, death.

The heart is actually two pumps, joined side by side, and working together in complete harmony, pumping the average adult's five litres of blood round the entire circulation every five minutes. The pumps each consist of two chambers separated by valves. The upper chambers receive the blood and the lower chambers pump it out. The right atrium, or upper chamber, receives the dark blood that is low in oxygen and high in carbon dioxide as it comes back from the rest of the body, and the right ventricle pumps it to the lungs. In the lungs the blood gives up its load of carbon dioxide and takes on a new supply of oxygen, which gives it a bright red colour. The left atrium receives the bright red oxygen-rich blood and the left ventricle pumps it round all the rest of the body, where it reaches every tissue by way of the 100,000 miles of blood vessels.

The coronary arteries

The heart has its own special circulation to supply the blood to its muscle tissue. These are the coronary arteries. By far the most common cardiovascular problem is coronary artery disease. In this disease, over the course of many years these arteries get blocked by fatty material, just as pipes fur up with calcium deposits in hard-water areas. It's a gradual process, often starting in childhood, and appreciable fatty streaks may be visible in the arteries by age twenty. By forty, the arteries may be 50% blocked. Usually there are no symptoms at all until an advanced stage is reached, for example a 70% blockage at age sixty. By now the heart may be unable to get enough oxygen for the extra work involved in physical exertion, like going up stairs or walking uphill, or with emotional stress. The first sign of trouble may be angina: pain or tightness in the chest in these situations. Other people are less fortunate, and their first symptom of trouble may be a heart attack, possibly a fatal one. A blockage can be due to the sudden spasm of an artery, or to a breakdown in the fatty lining causing a blood clot to form. If only a small area loses its blood supply, complete recovery is possible, but a larger area will take longer to heal and the heart may be left permanently weakened. A really large area of damage will prevent the heart from working at all, and death will result.

High blood cholesterol, high blood pressure and obesity are three related factors that are closely associated with cardiovascular disease. If the cholesterol level is high, other fats are likely to be high as well, and that means that the blood is relatively thick, sticky and viscous. This sort of blood needs more pressure to get it around the circulation, so the blood pressure tends to rise. Fatty deposits get left in the walls of the arteries and over the years they become narrower, which also necessitates a higher pressure to keep the blood circulating. Sticky blood at high pressure, going through narrow, clogged-up vessels, is a recipe for disaster. In addition, the overfilled fat-storage tissues need extra blood vessels, making another demand on the heart and blood pressure.

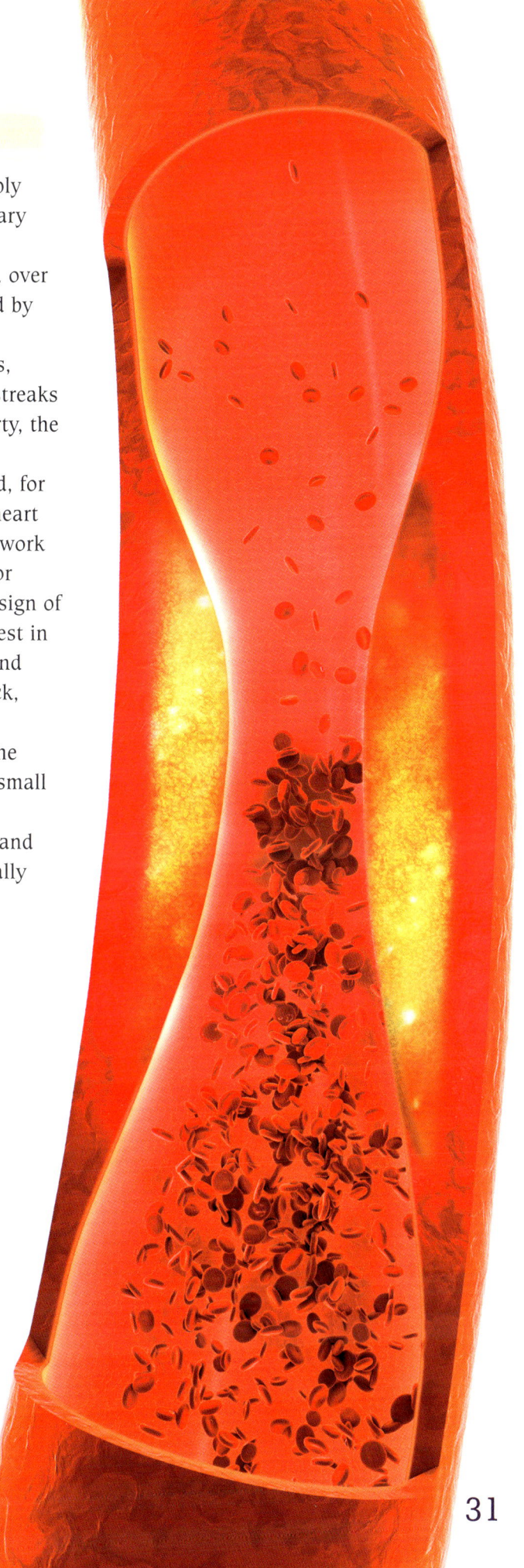

Cholesterol and the repair process

Why does the fatty material stick to the artery walls in the first place? Most disease processes can be shown to be attempts by the body to overcome abnormal situations. Atherosclerosis (*athero* means 'soggy' and describes the fatty material; *sclerosis* means 'hardening', referring to fibrous material) begins with a healing process: something has gone wrong and the body responds with inflammation in preparation for the healing process. A tiny damaged area in the lining of an artery is quickly repaired with a very thin layer of fatty material, which is then sealed in place with a very thin layer of fibre. The original damage to the artery wall could be due to some harmful substance in the circulating blood, or simply to a lack of vitamin C (a lack of vitamin C damages arterial walls). The cholesterol-rich patch is to protect and heal the damaged area and is designed to be temporary. If the conditions are not improved, the process continues repeatedly until the artery is almost completely blocked up. If, however, the wrong conditions are reversed, the arterial blockage can begin to reverse too. Although the coronary arteries get the most attention, the process can affect large and medium-sized arteries throughout the body.

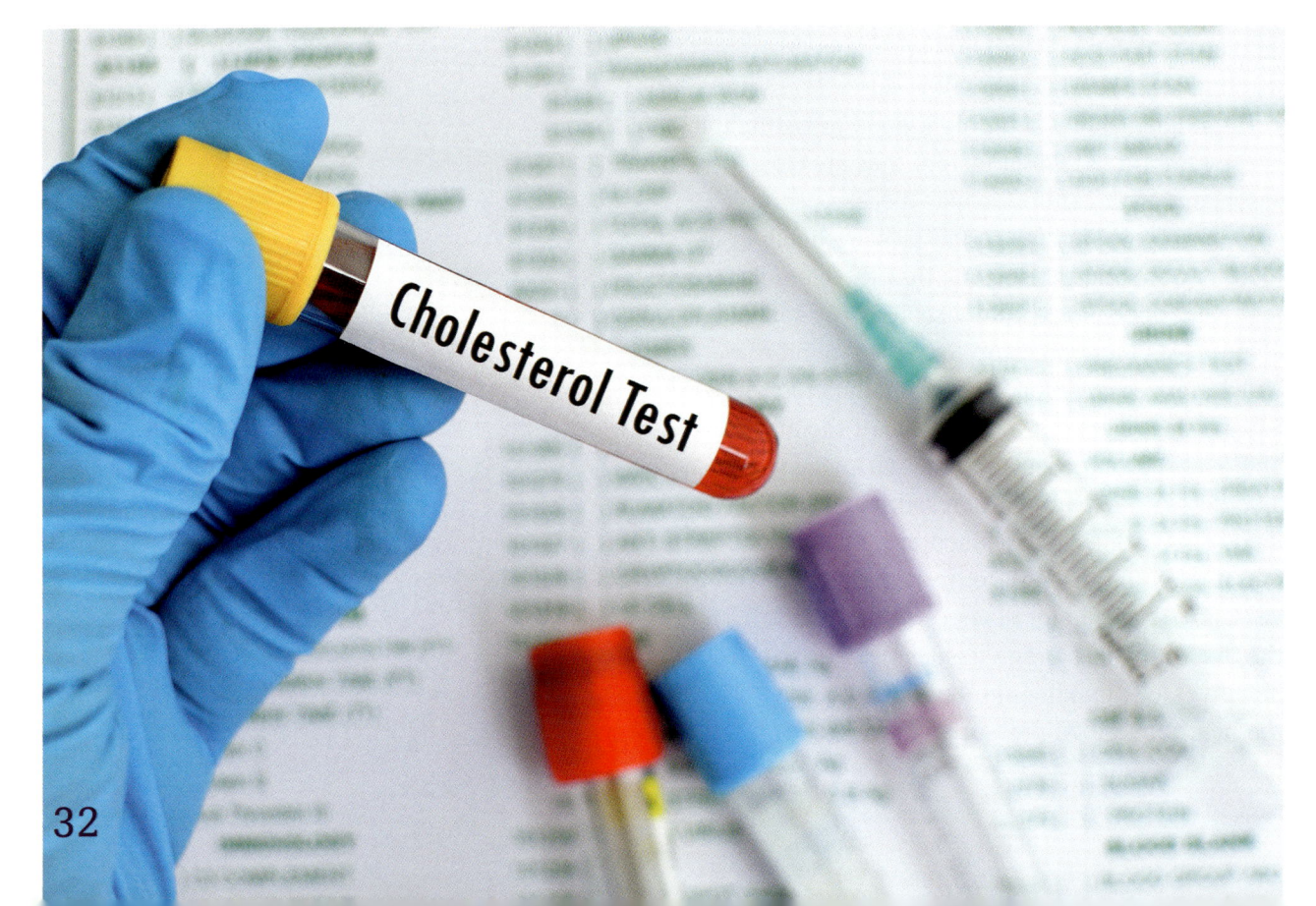

In the last half-century, enough research papers linking atherosclerosis to dietary fat and cholesterol have been published to fill a large warehouse. The conclusions of these papers consistently link coronary artery disease and the other degenerative arterial diseases with cholesterol and saturated fat intake. Cholesterol occurs in all animals, but does not occur in any plants. It is present in every animal cell and is present in every animal food product except egg white. (Eggs are enormous single cells, and the cholesterol is in the yolk.) Saturated fat is the prominent fat in mammals, including of course cows, sheep and pigs. The saturated fat is also present in their milk, which is one reason why ovo-lacto vegetarians (those who use milk and eggs) are not immune to heart disease. When saturated fat is present with cholesterol in the food, the blood level and arterial damage are worse than they would be if the cholesterol were associated with unsaturated fat, as it is in fish and poultry. The standard cholesterol-lowering diets emphasise limiting red meat, and using chicken and fish, and skimmed milk. These diets were worked out before it was understood that animal *protein* raises cholesterol levels, even in the absence of fat, which goes some way to explain why these diets have not been very successful. It is important to understand that fish and poultry do not, as many think, lower cholesterol levels; they actually raise them, but less so than red meat does.

High blood cholesterol and high blood pressure have been viewed as causes of heart disease, and treatment has been aimed at reducing their levels. But cholesterol is not the enemy: because it is part of the structure of all our cells, it's needed to repair all damaged cells. High blood cholesterol and high blood pressure are a response to the disease process, not the cause of it. To be successful, treatment has to go to the cause of the inflammation that starts the process off. Whatever the exact details of that, the role of lifestyle is clear: inactivity, faulty diet, smoking, alcohol and stress need to be dealt with. Although medications have their place, lifestyle changes are the route to lasting recovery.

Benefits of plant foods

Plant foods are the obvious choice for preventing and reversing arterial disease. They contain no cholesterol, and the fats they contain are predominantly unsaturated. They also contain fibre, which acts as a trap to remove cholesterol from the digestive tract before it is absorbed. A plant food diet is ideal in every way. It adds no cholesterol and little saturated fat to the blood, making it thinner and less likely to clot. This blood is much easier to pump around the system, so the blood pressure can be lower. As a plant food diet tends to be bulkier and more filling, it's lower in calories; and, if there is an increase in exercise as well, the fat stores can be reduced, along with the extra blood vessels they needed. This type of diet is also likely to be high in vitamin C, which is necessary for healthy arteries. An unrefined plant food diet will help to prevent cardiovascular disease by lowering blood cholesterol and blood pressure, and by helping to reduce weight. In fact, it is the only permanent way to reduce weight for many people. As it brings down the weight, it brings non-insulin-dependent diabetes (much the most common type) under control as well. In fact, you just can't lose with a natural, unrefined plant food diet.

Exercise

However, diet alone is not enough. In the West, most people just don't get enough exercise, and physically inactive people have around twice the risk of a heart attack when compared with those who are moderately or vigorously active. There is good evidence that regular and frequent moderately-intense exercise protects against heart attacks. Thirty minutes on at least five days each week is recommended. People who already have heart problems need to exercise too, within the limits of their illness. Walking is the best and safest all-round form of exercise. Exercise is most helpful when it is enjoyed, and also when it has a purpose, like gardening and other forms of active work.

Smoking

Tobacco is a major risk factor for cardiovascular disease. Smokers are ten times more likely to die before age sixty than non-smokers, and many of these deaths will be due to cardiovascular disease. The effects of tobacco smoking on the heart deserve a large section in this chapter, but, to save repetition, here is a summary: among the numerous poisons in tobacco smoke, nicotine seems to be the main culprit as far as the heart and blood vessels are concerned. Nicotine causes the blood vessels to contract, which in turn causes the blood pressure to rise. It also makes the heart muscle more irritable and more likely to beat irregularly. Smoking promotes the development of atherosclerosis, and also increases the tendency of the blood to clot. In addition to all this the carbon monoxide in tobacco smoke reduces the oxygen-carrying capacity of the blood by up to ten percent. This combination of effects is ideal for promoting coronary artery disease and other cardiovascular problems, and explains why smokers are so much more at risk than non-smokers.

Alcohol

Alcohol poses some tricky questions. 'The French paradox' has stimulated a vast amount of research, some of it sponsored by the drinks industry, to find out why the French, who are noted for their love of wine, have less coronary artery disease than others who drink much less. Compared with the UK the French live about a year longer; 31% of deaths in France are recorded as due to cardiovascular (heart and blood vessel) disease, compared to 34% in the UK; and they drink more than twice as much alcohol. A vast amount of research has been done to discover the reason for these small statistical advantages. Although heavy drinking causes some very serious heart problems, including life-threatening arrhythmias (irregular beats) and damage to the heart muscle fibres, some researchers claim that moderate drinking helps to prevent coronary artery disease. This is puzzling, because alcohol is a very potent cell poison, with a special affinity for the cells of the nervous system, and it seems unlikely that such a poison would actually have a protective effect on the heart. It's a very complex subject to research because so many different factors are involved, all of them difficult to measure exactly. It's true that there are some health-promoting properties in red wine, but they come from the red grape skins, not the alcohol.

Caffeine

Caffeine is also controversial, with experts able to quote research supporting both sides. Some have found links between caffeine, high blood pressure and coronary artery disease; others have not. Optimal health programmes avoid caffeine because of its ability to increase stress in general and insomnia in particular. Although there may be little hard evidence about caffeine and the heart, there is plenty of evidence about other harmful effects of this popular substance.

Social, psychological and spiritual factors

Social, psychological and spiritual factors are very important in preventing cardiovascular disease too. Fashions in psychology have changed over the years. The 'type A' person – aggressive, ambitious, intolerant, pushy, impatient, in a stressful, high-status position – was thought to have the highest risk of a heart attack. Then the dissatisfied, stressed-out, low-status workers were noticed to be even more at risk, and many people of all kinds succumb to heart attacks or strokes precipitated by severe emotional stress. 'Type B' people – calm, contented and laid back – were noticed to have the lowest risk.

One simple fact – very clear from a vast amount of research – is that optimists do far better than pessimists: they suffer less cardiovascular disease to start with and they recover more quickly if they do develop it. Psychological factors are perhaps the most important of all the factors in both prevention and cure of cardiovascular problems. As well as eating well, exercising well and avoiding poisons, it's vital to cultivate a peaceful and contented frame of mind. The most successful way to do this, in today's stressful world, is to develop trust in divine power. In the Gospel according to Matthew, chapter 11, verses 28 to 30 (here paraphrased), is Jesus' invitation to all who are stressed: 'Come to Me all you who are heavy laden and I will give you rest . . . learn of Me and you will find rest for your souls.' The Bible is a treasure chest of divine wisdom and comfort. And there is plenty of scientific evidence that religion is good for your health.

Clearing blocked arteries

There is more than one way to do this. **Angioplasty** is a method where a tube is actually passed into the blocked artery, under the guidance of ultrasound scanning. When the tube reaches the blocked area, it is inflated, clearing the blockage by squashing it flat against the artery wall. If this doesn't work, a stent (a tiny tube) can be inserted to keep the formerly blocked part open. Angioplasty can give immediate symptom relief, but because the cause of the atherosclerosis hasn't been removed the arteries almost always re-block, often within a year or so.

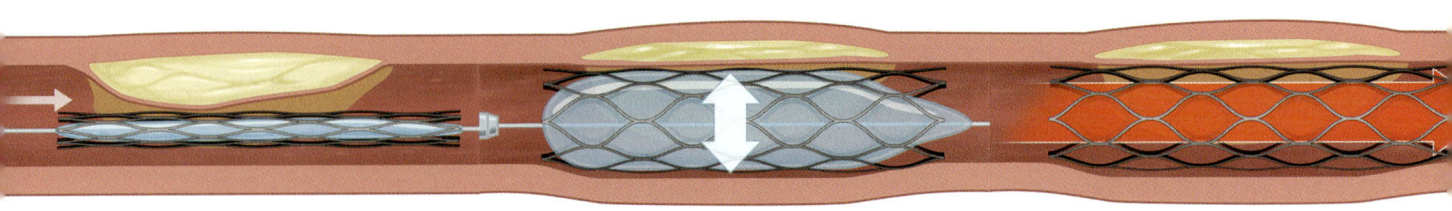

Coronary artery bypass surgery is now a very common operation in the Western world. Veins taken from the patient's leg are used to bypass the blocked areas of the coronary arteries. Between one and five grafts can be done. The immediate effects are very good, and patients feel better than they have done for years. The cardiac symptoms are relieved, but this surgery can have serious side effects, including strokes and other forms of brain damage – fortunately, usually to a minor extent, but often still enough to prevent the patient from resuming all their former activities. Even when the immediate results are excellent, unless the factors that caused the problem are changed, the grafts themselves are liable to block up within a few years. On the other hand, with an optimal health programme, the grafts can be expected to give many years of useful life.

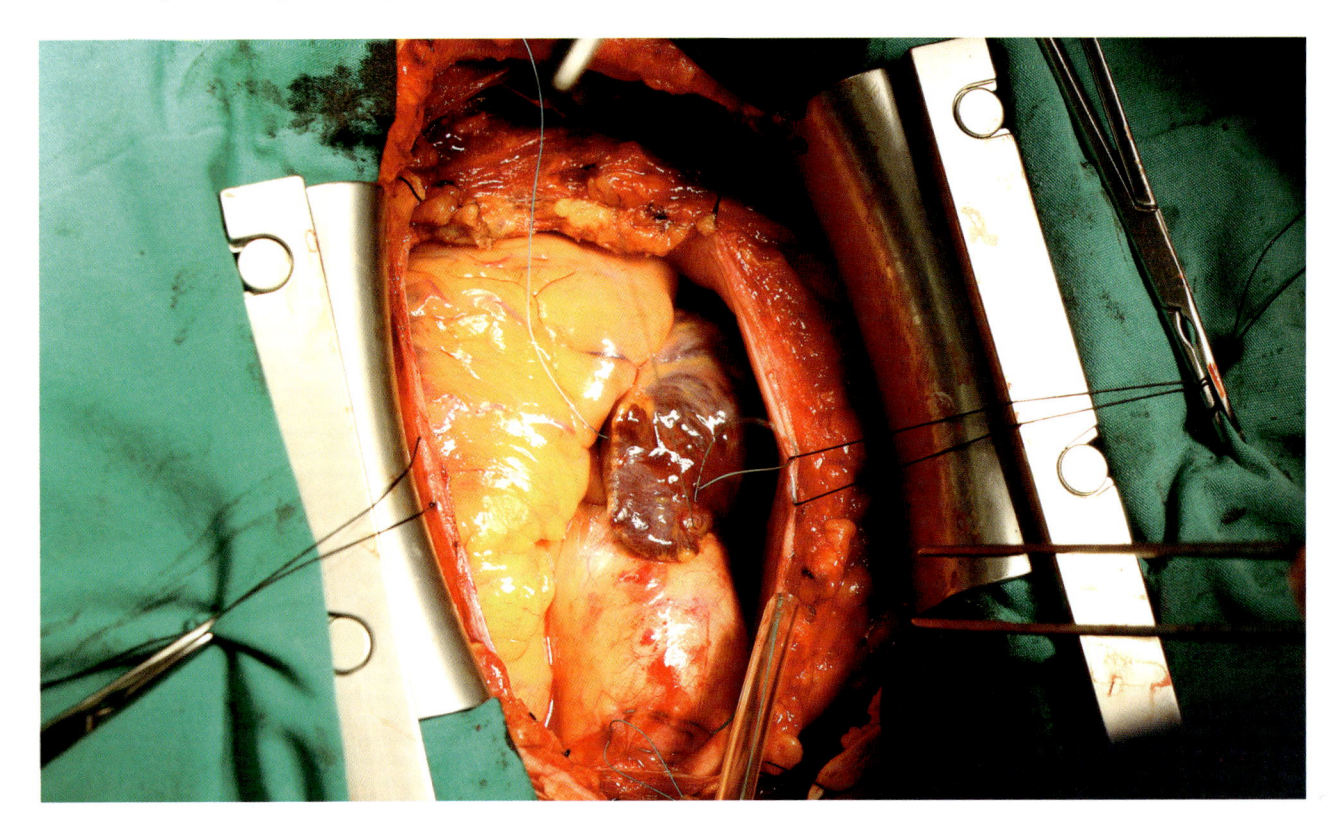

Reversing the damage

A much more satisfactory form of treatment is to remove the factors that caused the problem, and so start to reverse the disease process. As the disease may take a lifetime to develop, we should not be surprised that it takes a few years to reverse. The encouraging thing is that the benefits of disease reversal are felt long before the process is complete. In fact, symptoms of angina normally start to improve almost as soon as an optimal programme is started, and certainly the patient can expect to feel noticeably better after ten days.

Diet plays an important part in cardiovascular disease control. The standard heart diet, approved by the American and British heart foundations, could be described as a modified ordinary diet. Cholesterol is limited to 200mg a day, and fat is limited to 20% of the total calories, as opposed to the normal diet, with over 200mg of cholesterol, and nearer 40% of the calories from fat. This diet is no doubt better than the average one, but it doesn't go far enough to be really effective. It may slow down the disease process, but it certainly does not stop it. In one ten-year study, the arterial blockage had increased in 41% of patients after three years, and in 85% of patients after ten years, in patients following the heart foundation's guidelines.

The diet Dean Ornish used for his Lifestyle Heart Trial was very similar to the diet Nathan Pritikin used at his Longevity Research Institute. It consists mainly of unrefined plant foods: fruit, vegetables, wholegrain cereals and pulses, and a very small amount of skimmed milk products and egg white, adding up to 5mg of cholesterol a day and under 15% of the calories from fat. After one year on the Lifestyle Heart Trial diet, 84% of patients showed a measurable improvement, according to their angiograms. Their total cholesterol levels came down, the good HDL level rose, and the bad LDL level fell. Additional factors in the programme were stress management training and avoiding smoking, alcohol and caffeine – the latter not so much because of any direct effects on the heart, but because stress control was an important factor in the programme.

The diet at the Weimar Institute and its sister institutions goes further. It is 100% plant food, and therefore 100% cholesterol-free. As it's almost completely unrefined, a wide variety of seeds and nuts can be included, and even olives and avocados, without fear of there being too much fat. The average unrefined plant food diet provides most of its calories from carbohydrate (mainly as starch) and 10-15% each from protein and fat. This programme also produces very good results. It gives rapid relief of symptoms including angina, normalisation of blood pressure, blood cholesterol and blood sugar levels, and weight loss in the overweight. There are also good results with many other degenerative problems, such as diabetes and arthritis. This programme also includes vigorous exercise, encourages the use of water and sunlight as treatments, excludes the social poisons and has an optional Bible-based stress relief programme.

All really successful heart programmes include strong social and emotional support. Having a support network of caring friends or relatives can make all the difference between recovery and invalidism. Let's support our harassed and overworked friends, neighbours and family members, and help prevent some heart attacks. Nearly 200 scientific studies have been made of Seventh-day Adventists, to find the secret of their longer, healthier lives with their lower incidence of heart disease, strokes and cancer. One of the most important reasons may well be the strong social support that belonging to a comparatively small denomination gives; another is their weekly rest day; but really the strongest support they have comes from their belief in the kind and loving Heavenly Father who is in control of their lives.

[1] www.who.int/mediacentre/factsheets/fs310/en/index2.html
[2] www.ncbi.nlm.nih.gov/books/NBK45688

Useful information sources:
World Health Organisation
British Heart Foundation
American Heart Association

38

Stress: how it works

4

A medical student was shown the way into a huge cylinder. It was twenty feet long and sixteen feet in diameter. It was made of seven-inch armour plate. Inside he found a beautiful little furnished apartment where he would live for the next few days.

The apartment was carpeted throughout, with a small kitchen, a bed, a settee, chair, desk and reading lamp. The whole environment inside the sealed-off room (temperature, humidity, light and sound) could be controlled at the will of white-coated scientists. Special mirrors allowed observers to look in unnoticed, and elaborate sensors and wires monitored the responses in various parts of the young man's body.

The volunteer understood that the experiment he, and others, would participate in would demonstrate how we cope with changes in our environment. It was, however, much more than that. *It would demonstrate dramatically that our thoughts directly affect the health of our bodies.*

After he had settled into his new 'home' tests began. Information was recorded from the brain, heart and muscles. Not a muscle twitch, an alteration in body temperature, or the slightest tensing of his body went unnoticed.

A loudspeaker made it possible for the student to listen to the conversation of the staff outside the chamber. What he did not realise was that much of what seemed to be idle conversation was deliberately planned. One day, for instance, as he was lying in bed, his eyes closed, a doctor was chatting to another doctor and said something like, 'Did you write that letter you promised your wife?' Immediately the muscles that would hold a pen tightened in the student's hand. Later, when the conversation was about walking, the muscles of ambulation tensed.

39

The doctors went from one part of the body to another observing similar responses. They knew that the student was listening to every word they said, even though he appeared to be sound asleep.

On another occasion while they chatted outside the chamber, one of the men asked: 'How did the medical students do in the examination?' This student had taken the examination referred to and, immediately, there was generalised tension. 'Oh, they did terribly,' came the reply, and with that the student's blood pressure rose, his heart beat faster and his respiration rhythm changed. The doctors went on to talk about another subject – and then came in with the *coup de grâce*. They discussed a certain young lady that this boy was courting, or trying to court, and as soon as her name was mentioned his blood pressure rose significantly, his heart rate changed, his breathing became uneven and shallow and, when the doctor said, 'Yes, I met her last evening, she was out with so and so' . . . he hit the jackpot!

The scientists who conducted this, and many similar experiments, found that every thought and feeling is reflected in the reactions of the physical organism. On your way to the shops or to work tomorrow morning look at the people around you. How many of them look tense and drawn; how many over the age of 25 are smiling and really happy? Most of them will have developed an unnecessary sense of urgency. Rushing around when they could walk, and driving as if on a race track. You've heard of road rage. Our lives were never meant to be lived in the constant state of tension that is so common today.

We are in a world of iPhones, laptops and tablets, all loaded with the latest social media. The pace is fast-forward. Life is exacting. But with all the advantages of Westernised, urban living comes stress, and almost everyone suffers from it at some time.

Stress is simply the body's reaction to the wear and tear of life. Every single activity in which we engage and emotion we feel – whether it's asking the boss for a pay increase, getting badly sunburned or suffering loss of sleep – sets up stress. The way your body reacts to such stress agents or *stressors* has much to do with your immediate health and your potential for a long life.

We must remember, however, that individual vulnerability to stress varies widely, and whereas one person can adjust to changes in lifestyle, others will crumble under the same circumstances. Indeed, we should remember that stress is a very essential part of life. In its simplest form it means 'stimulation' and therefore it can be perfectly true that many people work better 'under pressure', as we say.

Stress can often be the spice of life. Our bodies and our minds were built to take stress and to thrive on it. The occasional shock of adrenaline can also be a great cure for boredom and indifference. When handled well, stress gives us added motivation to overcome obstacles and brings us strength to handle threatening situations which might damage or destroy our happiness, our homes, our safety or our self-esteem. The problem comes with overload.

Beyond a certain level, which is different for every individual, stress becomes destructive. Intense and persistent anger, fear, frustration or worry can threaten health. It is this build-up of stress without release of tension which leads to trouble. We need to know the limits of our abilities, beyond which we reap negative and harmful results.

Actually, it is not the stress itself that is so important and dangerous, so much as the mental and physical response that we make to what Hamlet called 'the thousand natural shocks that flesh is heir to'. Biochemists have established the importance of stress in connection with coronary heart disease. The adrenaline that is pumped into the system by all our shocks, worries and anxieties would have been used up naturally years ago by sheer hard work. In civilised society we tend to stifle our impulses, and take very little exercise. Our adrenaline increases the heart rate and blood pressure, increases the output of blood fats, and increases blood concentration. Lack of exercise and hard work to burn off the chemical effects of our tensions and worries is one of the major reasons why coronary heart disease is the number-one killer in society today.

In a similar way, we realise that when Uncle Harry is in hospital with his ulcers it is largely due to the excessive pressures of work at his office, or to worries about his family. The more mechanised and 'uptight' we become, the greater the problem.

A suitable definition of the optimal stress level has still to be formulated, because what one person finds stressful others enjoy – some among the population are 'stress seekers' while others are 'stress copers'. Some prefer a peaceful, untroubled, routine life, while others seek out problems to solve and challenges to meet. Most of us are extremely fearful of heights but there are those 'stress seekers' who like to climb mountains or take part in free-fall parachuting or bungee jumping. To them this is exhilarating. But they may not want to go potholing! Stress is a friend or foe according to the personality of the one experiencing it. The overall facts are, however, that the effects of population explosion, along with the development of a highly technological society, computerisation and the mass media, take their toll. Add to this the enormous increase of marital breakdown; the ever-widening generation gaps; economic crises; job dissatisfaction or loss – and you have a recipe for stress. Under such circumstances most of us are 'stress copers' doing our best to keep our heads above water.

The first signs that one is not coping with stress can be excessive tiredness, irritability, inefficiency at work or at home, and depression, after which the body will break down at its weakest point. Some people get severe headaches, others backaches, skin rashes, bowel disorders or severe indigestion. These, however, are only the warning signs, which if disregarded can lead to serious problems like stomach ulcers and coronary disease. Chronic hypertension, chronic fatigue syndrome, burnout/breakdowns and heart attacks easily follow.

Dr John Tomlinson, who presented a television documentary on stress, said: 'The problem is getting people to recognise that these symptoms are caused by mental strain and not some mysterious "bug".'

One of the first times these harmful effects were appreciated was when a young Canadian hunter was injured in a shooting accident and taken to a nearby army post where his wounds were tended. The shotgun blast left a hole in his side and stomach that never healed. This fistula made it possible for Doctor Beaumont, who attended him, to observe the digestive process in his stomach. For a number of years Dr Beaumont fed pieces of food to the patient and watched digestion in action. By and large his patient was co-operative and, while he was in a placid state of mind, the doctor noticed that the stomach lining was a fresh pink colour. On the other hand, when he was fearful or shocked, it became pale and starved of blood. At times of anger it would appear red and inflamed and would even break out in tiny haemorrhages. This was the beginning of a new area of medical science which some researchers claim points out the possible underlying reason for as much as nine-tenths of our illnesses.

Many years ago it was said, 'The relation that exists between the body and the mind is very intimate. When one is affected, the other sympathises. The condition of the mind affects the health to a far greater degree than many realise. Many of the diseases from which men suffer are the result of mental depression. Grief, anxiety, discontent, remorse, guilt, distrust, all tend to break down the life forces and to invite decay and death.'[1]

In Britain there are counselling services for teachers, just as there are for the members of many other professions. However, it would appear that teachers require far more counselling than other professionals. Their counselling service is used far more. In addition, there is a greater degree of absenteeism through illness among teachers than among any other professional group. It is accepted that the stress levels in teaching are higher than those in most, if not all, other professions.

Studies have been done on the effects of stress in a variety of social contexts. Phenomena as diverse as road rage, child abuse, and high rates of drug and alcohol abuse have all been linked to rising stress levels.

Enough of the nature and dangers of stress; what we really want to know is how to cope with it.

Life's bank account

One of the most important discoveries in recent years is that each person is born with a certain amount of vital force which must last him or her for a lifetime. The amount varies from person to person. Professor Hans Selye, a pioneer in stress research, gathered together a vast number of medical studies which described the body's reaction to just about every conceivable type of stress. He discovered what he termed a 'bank account' of nervous energy and wrote: 'It is as though at birth each individual inherits a certain amount of adaptation energy, the magnitude of which is determined by his genetic background. There is just so much of it and we must budget accordingly.'[2]

In other words, we can make withdrawals of nervous energy at will but we can never increase the vital force we receive at birth by making deposits. The only control we have over this precious treasure is the rate at which we make our withdrawals. Those who tend to be 'spendthrifts' will soon find themselves in difficulty. Many people believe that after they have exposed themselves to stressful activities a rest can restore them to where they were before, but this is false. Experiments on animals have shown clearly that each exposure to stress leaves an indelible scar and uses up reserves of vital force that cannot be replaced. However, there is much we can do to improve our situation and maintain our bank balance.

Get away from it all

If you recognise that you are a stress sufferer, one of the best things you can do is to take a complete break from your normal routine. There are differing opinions as to how long that 'complete break' should be. Some advocate frequent short breaks while others advocate a minimum of two or three weeks taken in one stretch. If you are the kind of person who worries about packing, crowded airports and overbooked package holidays, don't plan your three weeks overseas, even if it is in the sun. Learn, too, from those people who come back from their holidays looking like dishcloths – because they have travelled thousands of miles in the car 'doing' this place or that, and have spent every night at a rave or a disco!

The whole purpose of a holiday is to relax and get away from the stresses and strains of life. This year, why not plan to find a small hotel or caravan in some beauty spot where you can *really* unwind, or take a boat and cruise gently up a canal or river? You will be surprised what a difference it will make. Come to think of it, you might save some extra stress that could result from overspending on a luxury holiday.

For most of us holidays may come just once or twice a year. In between these breaks, try to build into your diary other days out, or weekends with friends and family that can be looked forward to and enjoyed.

Learn to loaf a little

It took a war to teach us that we need to balance our work with relaxation. During the Battle of Britain military production was given the highest priority, and in one aircraft factory employees were scheduled to work seventy-four hours a week – they were pressed to the limit. In fact, the management, aware of high absenteeism and deteriorating morale, decided that they would try lowering the required time by ten hours from seventy-four hours to sixty-four hours a week. They were pleasantly surprised to find that production levels remained exactly the same as before. This made them decide to experiment further. After a few weeks the required work hours were further reduced by ten to fifty-four hours a week. As a result production – which was previously thought to be 100% – went up by 15%, and along with it the morale of the workers improved. There was less spoiled work, fewer accidents and less absenteeism.

We have the war to thank for our traditional tea break. It was found that workers improved in efficiency when introduced to a ten-minute break in the mornings and the afternoons. In some factories workers were even provided with a roll of paper on which to lie down and catnap as well. This may sound 'way out', but many business people today are finding this to be the answer to their stress problems, and are not ashamed to put their heads down once in a while or even stretch full-length on a carpeted floor. Ten minutes later they are ready for anything!

Rest is the stuff of which long life is made. It can be gained in any quiet place. Give yourself cushions of time. Stress diseases are the so-called hurry-worry ills that usually result from too tight a schedule. Such pressure leads to slip-ups, accidents and injuries. Take time for yourself, lean back on your bed, prop up on two pillows and read a good book. Forget clocks, calendars, appointments, problems and debts. This time is just for you – and your body – to help you unwind and make your day a nicer one and your life a longer one.

Get plenty of sleep

It has been shown that animals die more quickly from lack of sleep than from lack of food. Sufficient sleep is vital for nervous stability. The amount recommended by doctors varies with age, ranging from fifteen hours between three and five years, to seven or eight hours for an adult. To get a good night's sleep one should go to bed regularly at the same time and not too late. Don't let the attractions of television or other excitement shorten the time when you ought to be asleep. Nothing will age you faster, or burn the reserves in your energy bank more quickly, than loss of sleep.

Sleep is one of nature's most effective restorers, not only physically, but mentally. It sweeps away fatigue and helps us retain our mental balance.

This short explanation may help you to understand why stress appears when there is sleep deprivation due to alteration in shift duties and other commitments, or when the family, and particularly the mother, is disturbed night after night by the nocturnal activities of babies or children.

Exercise with care

For many people it doesn't help to suggest that they get plenty of sleep if insomnia is part of their problem. This too could be due to the build-up of adrenaline in their systems, and a little regular exercise which stretches the big muscles could be the answer to a good night's sleep as well as breaking the vicious chain of stress. If you have felt tension building up at the office or in the home, you owe it to yourself to balance work with play. Sports centres have become popular places to spend a lunch hour or evening. Choose an exercise or a sport that you will enjoy, and preferably something that you can continue in good or bad weather. Badminton, bowling, gardening, hiking, climbing, walking and swimming all have their benefits as adrenaline-discharging activities.

Talk about troubles

You've heard it a score of times, 'A trouble shared is a trouble halved.' It always helps to get worries off your chest by confiding in a sympathetic friend. When serious problems start to get you down, don't be afraid to discuss them with your family doctor, your pastor, minister or priest, or an understanding member of your family. Gloomy, angry, unkind and selfish thoughts bottled up in your mind cause the neurons in the area of the brain called the hypothalamus to fire nervous impulses to the pituitary glands that lie just below the brain, helping them to produce the growth hormone (GH or HGH). This stimulates the adrenal glands, located slightly above the kidneys, to produce special hormones that cause the blood pressure to rise, the heart to beat faster and the muscles to tune up in order to escape danger from without the body or attack an infection or toxin within. When a surge of these hormones is caused by continuous negative thinking their effect can be very harmful.

On the other hand, when our thoughts are calm and tender, the hypothalamus sends forth impulses that cause the pituitary gland to secrete a chemical called ACTH, which, in turn, causes the adrenal glands to secrete cortisone and other substances. These substances have the effect of returning blood pressure and heart rate to normal. An improved blood supply aids the processes of digestion, elimination and assimilation, and, as a result, we have a feeling of peace, relaxation and optimism.

If we are Christians we are able to discuss our troubles with God, who always hears and cares.

Hobbies and pastimes

Before the days of television and other forms of mass entertainment – which tend to increase our stress factors – people spent their evenings and leisure hours in conversation, music and reading. A good creative hobby is an extremely effective prescription against stress. People who can lose their day-to-day worries and responsibilities in art, model-building, stamp collecting, embroidery, basketry, candle-making and a host of other pastimes are fortunate indeed. One wonders, however, how many more potential sculptors, potters, flautists and dressmakers there might be among those who carry their troubles home with them in a briefcase, or who long for peace of mind night after night in front of the 'box'?

Hydrotherapy and massage

There is nothing like a warm bath, foaming with pine essence, to relax you at the end of a long day. Water can be used both to stimulate and to relax the body. A cold mitten friction can tone up the system in the morning and a warm bath or shower can prepare you for bed at night. A warm hot water bottle behind the neck will complete your comfort.

Another very effective procedure is the hot foot-bath. This is valuable because of its effect on the entire circulation of the body. By dilating the blood vessels in the feet and legs it relieves congestion in other parts of the body.

Habits and an orderly way of life

By the time a child knows how to cycle, the movements necessary to maintain balance have become reflexes and no longer require the conscious effort that caused the nerves to become tired and tense in order to maintain that balance. Reflex actions take far less nervous energy than those requiring a conscious effort. For repeated actions to become automatic you must have orderliness. For example, if a working man is to do his job efficiently his hand should always be able to find the same tool available in the same place. Whatever your task, orderliness and planned actions will help calm your nerves.

Seek some peace and quiet

The constant noise of machines, cars, trucks and trains; the constant ringing of telephones; and the noise of the radio and television, fray the nerves. Many people sleep through noises that they have become accustomed to but the brain still registers them. This is supported by the fact that if a noise to which we are accustomed, such as a ticking clock, stops we suddenly wake up.

A British government committee on noise reported that there was no doubt that noise affects our health and is responsible for tension and speedy fatigue. Noise is measured in decibels from 1, which is the point at which hearing begins, to 120, which is the level at which the human body feels pain. The rustling of leaves may register at 10 decibels, while a noisy motorcycle or scooter can be 80-90 decibels. Have you thought that noise could contribute to your tensions? If you cannot avoid it at work, at least balance your life with intervals of peace and quiet in the countryside or at home, and if you live by a noisy road or railway line, double or triple glazing may be a very valuable investment for your health's sake.

Eat well

Even our diet can affect the stress that we suffer. Processed food, especially refined carbohydrates in the form of white-flour products and too much sugar, robs the body of essential vitamins from the B range, which are the basic ingredients for a healthy nervous system.

Almost everyone who is suffering from nervous exhaustion is deficient in the B vitamins. For most people today who eat peeled, boiled and fried packaged convenience foods in a hurry, there is need to restore the B vitamins. This can be done by supplementing with a B complex or with Brewer's Yeast tablets. Better still, eating wholewheat bread and cereals rich in B vitamins will help restore our energy levels.

Relaxation techniques

Finally, here are a few important relaxation techniques.
For a loosening exercise sit on an armless chair or stool and lean slightly forwards so that your arms dangle. Shake your hands hard as though shaking off water. Imagine you are a string puppet and your shoulders are being pulled as high as possible – then cut the strings and allow them to fall. Pretend that you are carrying two heavy suitcases and feel your shoulders being pulled down, then drop the cases and relax. Afterwards roll your shoulders gently forwards six times and then backwards six times. Then pretend that your neck is broken and let your head drop forwards. Imagine it becoming heavier. Then slowly raise it. Repeat several times.

To relax muscles deliberately is more difficult than to contract them and it can seem almost impossible for a beginner. However, there is an inbuilt law of the body whereby, when one muscle group is deliberately tensed, the subconscious mind simultaneously relaxes the opposite group of muscles to permit the contraction to occur. We can use this law to our advantage by voluntarily contracting an opposing group of muscles so that those muscles and nerves that are commonly tensed become relaxed. To do this, either lie down – preferably with a low pillow and a pad or cushion under the hollow of your neck and back, and under your thighs – or sit straight in a chair. When you are comfortable, concentrate first on your feet and ankles and, as far as possible, tense them up by screwing in the toes and lifting the foot. After a few moments, stop and relax, registering the feelings of your relaxed feet in your brain. In the same way, tense your calf muscles, followed by those in your upper legs and buttocks.

Gradually work through the body, trunk, shoulders, arms, neck and head, deliberately tensing and straining each part in turn, concentrating on the feel of tension, then relaxing and registering the effect of this part of your body at rest.

Anatomical studies tell us that there is an intricate system of conductive fibres called nerves which serve, largely through the intermediation of the brain, to integrate the various organs of the body. These nerves carry impulses by a mechanism similar to that by which electric wires carry electrical impulses.

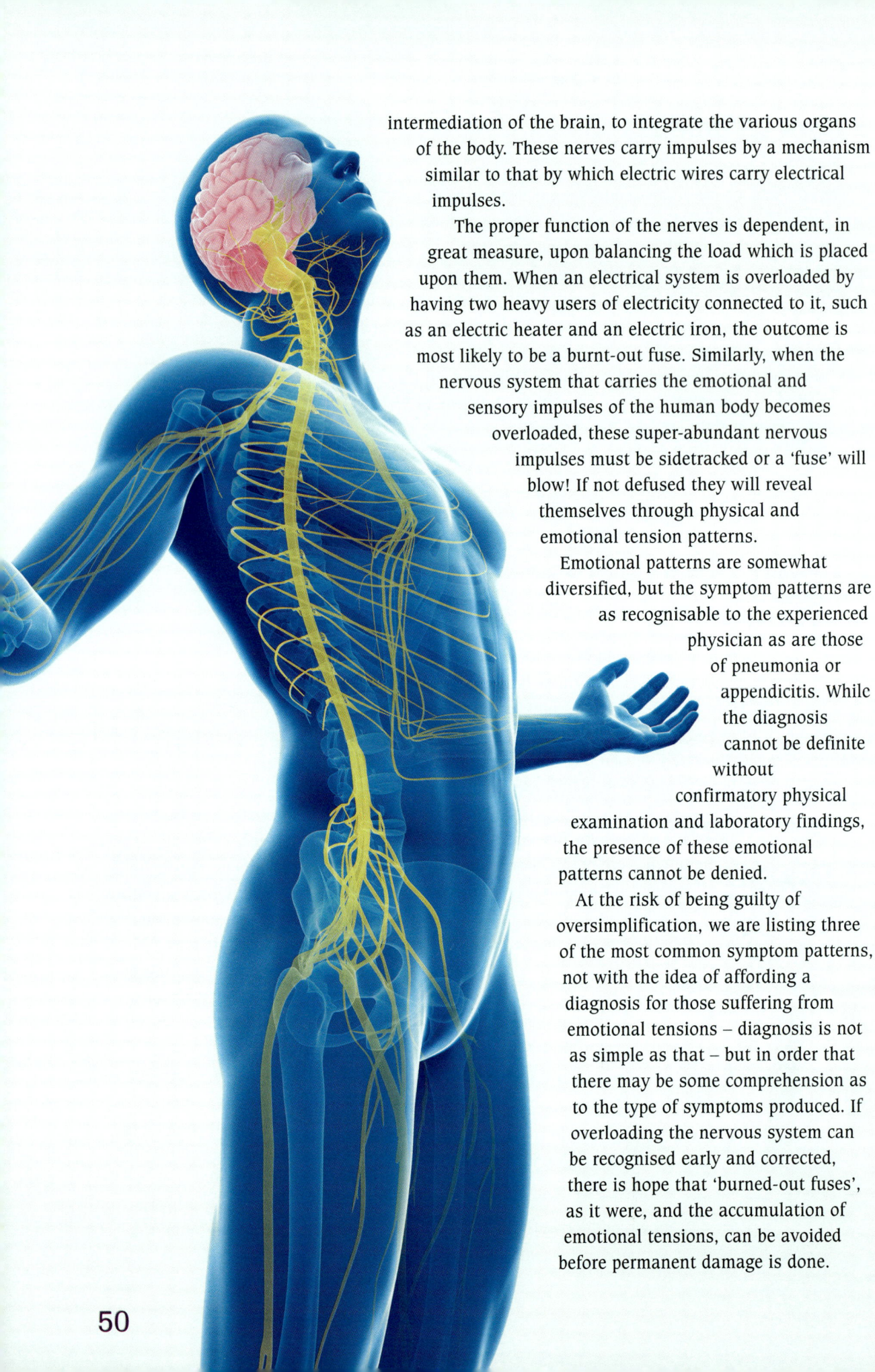

The proper function of the nerves is dependent, in great measure, upon balancing the load which is placed upon them. When an electrical system is overloaded by having two heavy users of electricity connected to it, such as an electric heater and an electric iron, the outcome is most likely to be a burnt-out fuse. Similarly, when the nervous system that carries the emotional and sensory impulses of the human body becomes overloaded, these super-abundant nervous impulses must be sidetracked or a 'fuse' will blow! If not defused they will reveal themselves through physical and emotional tension patterns.

Emotional patterns are somewhat diversified, but the symptom patterns are as recognisable to the experienced physician as are those of pneumonia or appendicitis. While the diagnosis cannot be definite without confirmatory physical examination and laboratory findings, the presence of these emotional patterns cannot be denied.

At the risk of being guilty of oversimplification, we are listing three of the most common symptom patterns, not with the idea of affording a diagnosis for those suffering from emotional tensions – diagnosis is not as simple as that – but in order that there may be some comprehension as to the type of symptoms produced. If overloading the nervous system can be recognised early and corrected, there is hope that 'burned-out fuses', as it were, and the accumulation of emotional tensions, can be avoided before permanent damage is done.

Three common tension patterns

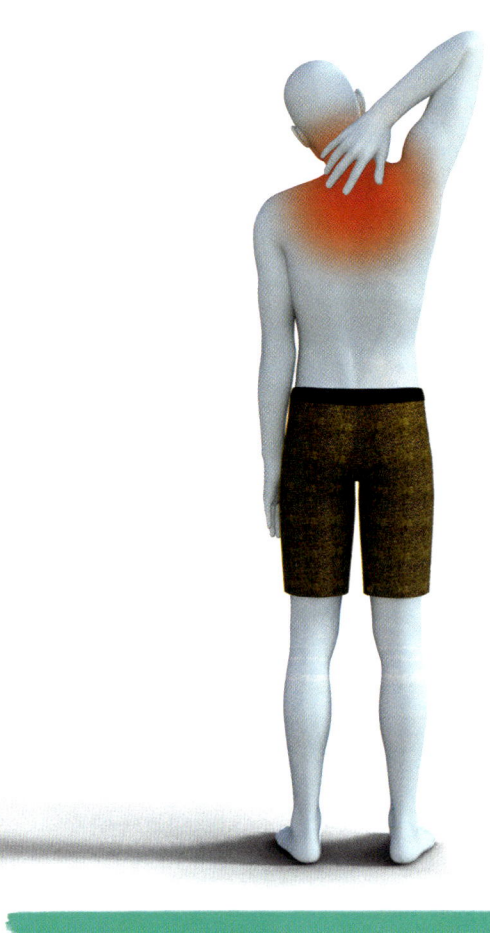

1 The stiff-neck tension pattern is characterised by painfully contracted muscles in the back of the neck. From here the pain may extend upwards to the top of the head and the forehead, in the form of a headache; downwards into the trapezius muscles, which are located above and between the shoulder blades; and/or forwards to produce a tense feeling in the throat.

It may appear that this muscular tension is caused by 'lack of backbone' in dealing with problems. The person becomes tense and apprehensive and often there is sleep disturbance. Paradoxically, what may have started as a lack of backbone may eventually lead to a stubborn, unbending attitude such as characterised the Israelites under Moses, who were called 'a stiff-necked people'. For this reason, these sufferers often become especially hard to help because they cannot see their way clear to accepting the explanations of their symptom pattern, nor can they readily alter their ways once the pattern becomes firmly established.

2 The chest-tension pattern consists of complaints that mainly involve the chest, such as conscious (and sometimes rapid) beating of the heart; discomfort over the heart region which may even be described as pain; a feeling that the chest is being squeezed as in a vice; and laboured breathing even when no obvious exertion has preceded it.

Physiologists point out that this is largely due to an imbalance of the nerves of the heart – between the nerves that put the brakes on the heart being understimulated and the nerves that speed the heart being overstimulated. Perhaps the term 'losing heart' best expresses this, for the heart is running away with itself as it were, as the driver's foot presses more firmly on the accelerator. Once the driver's foot is transferred from the accelerator to the brake, relief follows almost instantaneously. These sufferers are often fairly easily relieved of their complaints, once the cause is pointed out, even though they may initially be quite convinced that they have real 'heart trouble'. This relief is often accomplished by resolving those anxieties that have been plaguing the patient – literally allowing them to get it 'off their chests'!

Stomach-tension pattern, often referred to as 'nervous indigestion', is characterised by a feeling of bloating after eating, a sensation of inward tension in the abdomen. These symptoms correspond to what happens when the stomach is filled beyond its functional capacity. Interestingly enough, they are produced in the stomach when the emotions reach a state and type of tension such as we might describe by the term 'fed up'. The emotional tensions that affect the stomach are often those of resentfulness and bitterness. These tensions may at times be rather tenacious, but the temporary relief of their symptoms can quite easily be obtained through medicines that tend to re-establish the nervous balance of the stomach. If permanent relief is to be obtained, though, it is usually necessary to deal with the resentful and unforgiving spirit: otherwise ulceration may eventually result.

Admittedly, this is an over-simplification of tension patterns. These patterns may coexist or change from one into the other. There are also other possible tension patterns – for instance, those involving the skin, the lower bowel (colon), or the bladder. Our purpose in describing these tension patterns has been largely to emphasise that the causes of emotional tension must be dealt with quickly, otherwise the symptoms may continue to impair patients' health and lead them to contract an even more serious disease.[3]

Rhythmic breathing also calms and soothes mind and body. The 'in-breath' is a sign of tension, as, also, is breath holding. Think of the gasp of fear or pain. On the other hand the 'out-breath' is relaxing. Think of a sigh or the second half of a yawn. Breathing exercises are another aid to overcoming stress. Simply sit or lie completely relaxed and, without any strain or effort, take six leisurely, pleasurable breaths. Imagine that someone is pouring air into you and filling your chest just comfortably full, no more. Keep the breathing pattern rhythmic with the accent on the relaxing outward breath. Women who practise psycho-prophylaxis, which is largely based on breathing patterns, have found it possible to come through one of the most stressful experiences of their lives, childbirth, without the need of oxygen, gas or any other anaesthetics, completely conscious and completely relaxed.

Perfect peace

When our minds are ill at ease we also suffer physically, spiritually, mentally and socially, but, with a change for the better in our mental attitudes, as we learn to cope with stress, all the other dimensions that make us whole beings are equally strengthened.

There is one source of peace that we neglect at our peril. One Bible writer says this about the peace that comes from perfect trust in God: 'You will keep in perfect peace all who trust in you, all whose thoughts are fixed on you!' (Isaiah 26:3, NLT.) Jesus promised all His followers 'peace in Me'. He continued, 'Here on earth you will have many trials and sorrows. But take heart, because I have overcome the world.' (John 16:33, NLT.)

[1] E. G. White, *Ministry of Healing*, page 241
[2] *The Stress of Life*, page 15
[3] Paul E. Randolph, MD, FACS, *Release From Tension*, pages 19-23

A new approach to eating

A new way of eating is vital for anyone who is suffering from any of the degenerative diseases, or at risk of developing them. The same basic principles apply, whether one is anxiously waiting for coronary bypass surgery, struggling with non-insulin-dependent diabetes, wanting to lose weight and avoid such problems in the future, or simply wanting to feel fitter and enjoy life more.

Principle 1 • What to eat: choose whole plant food that contains 100% of its nutrients. As well as providing optimum nutrition, this gives a sense of satisfaction that is lacking when mainly refined foods are used. For weight-watchers it removes the need to count calorics.

Principle 2 • When to eat: eat meals at regular intervals, preferably five or six hours apart, with the last meal several hours before bedtime and with no food between meals. Plan to eat a moderately large breakfast and lunch, and a small, light evening meal. This regime makes it much easier to avoid extra calories.

Principle 3 • Make major changes in diet and lifestyle gradually, unless they are medically urgent. Rapid weight loss usually leads to rapid weight regain. A steady small loss, even as little as half a pound a week, is to be preferred. It's easier to maintain, and it doesn't throw the metabolism into starvation mode.

Principle 4 • Remember that the whole lifestyle is important, including exercise, avoiding poisons and staying cheerful.

Starvation mode

A sudden drop in calorie intake can throw the metabolism into starvation mode: the body gets the message that starvation is imminent, so every possible calorie of energy is conserved. Activity levels fall, and the weight just doesn't go down. As soon as any food is eaten, the fat storage cells go into emergency action and store every molecule they can get hold of, with disastrous effects on the weight-loss programme.

To avoid starvation mode, 1 have a consistent programme of vigorous daily exercise. This will ensure that the metabolism is more active and it will continue to burn up extra energy for hours after the exercise is over; 2 eat enough whole, unrefined plant food to satisfy the appetite; and 3 give up counting calories!

Fasting

Why fast? Fasting is a valuable tool in the treatment of many degenerative diseases. It can also be a helpful part of a weight-control programme, but prolonged fasting is counterproductive, as well as dangerous. When the body goes into starvation mode, it starts to burn up muscle tissue as well as fat, and calcium is removed from the bones.

For how long? Short fasts of up to 48 hours can be useful for developing the self-discipline necessary for lifestyle change, and also for developing a good appetite for a different type of food. 'Hunger is the best sauce,' as the old French proverb says.

How to fast? A really strong-minded person might choose to have a day or two on only water and herbal teas. Another might choose 24 hours on fruit and vegetable juices. Then there is the fruit fast – one or more days on only fruit at meal times, and only water between meals.

Another way of fasting is to change to a two-meal-a-day programme, omitting the evening meal. This kind of fasting can be continued indefinitely, but more rigorous programmes should not be continued for more than a few days without medical advice, particularly if there are serious health problems.

Starchy foods

You need them! Don't restrict bread, potatoes and other starchy foods unduly. Unrefined starches like wholemeal bread and potatoes baked in their skins are low-calorie foods – as long as they are not served with high-fat trimmings. Add butter or margarine and you double the calories. These foods are satisfying because they add bulk. They also help to prevent constipation, which is often a problem on the old-fashioned calorie-restricted slimming diets. Remember that unrefined starches are basic to healthy, whole-food diets.

A new start to menu planning

General guidelines

Unrefined starches are important for most meals: bread and cereals for breakfast, bread and/or starchy vegetables for dinners or main meals, bread to add substance to light meals.

Add generous amounts of fruits or vegetables and smaller amounts of high-protein plant foods like beans and lentils, or even smaller amounts of nuts and seeds.

Keep each meal fairly simple, without too many different types of food – but, from day to day and week to week, have as wide a variety of healthy, whole plant foods as you can.

Specific meal suggestions

Breakfast – fruit with cereals, bread and a spread makes a good, sustaining start to the day.

Once you get used to eating more **fruit**, it's difficult to get too much. Start the meal with one or more pieces of fresh fruit, and use fruit spread on bread, and fruit, fresh or dried, with breakfast cereals.

Cereals – this word doesn't only mean the packaged type from the supermarket or health food shop, but also granola that can be made at home and porridge that can be made from various types of grains, as well as the traditional oatmeal. Cereals are usually eaten with milk, but taste very good with fruit, raw or cooked, fruit juice, or non-dairy milks like soya or cashew. Porridge is good topped with something chewy like granola, chopped nuts or raisins, and there are few cereals that don't benefit from the addition of sliced banana. Bananas are a starchy fruit which is very nutritious and they can make a good meal on their own.

Breads – it's good to ring the changes with breads, too, now that wheat sensitivities are becoming so common. Have breads made with more than one type of grain, and use rye or other crispbreads as well.

Spreads – people who are overweight or have other serious health problems will want to avoid butter, and even margarine – which, after all, is only made from refined vegetable oils – and even the 'low fat' varieties are still only fat. So what should be spread on bread? Whole-food spreads are best. One-hundred-percent-nutritious 'butters' are made from whole nuts or seeds. These may be expensive to buy, but can be made quite cheaply at home.

So far as jams are concerned, ordinary ones are over 50% white sugar, but you can safely indulge your sweet tooth if you make your own whole-food jams with fresh or dried fruit.

Beans and lentils, nuts and seeds can all be used to make delicious savoury spreads.

Many people prefer savoury breakfasts, and these are good when whole foods are used.

57

Lunch/dinner – this is a main meal, and ideally should be at midday.

Choose a starchy basis – potatoes, rice, pasta, millet and so on.

Add generous servings of vegetables; some cooked, some raw.

Add some high-protein plant foods too. These could be beans or lentils added to a vegetable stew, or could be a separate dish.

Dessert? Keep it small and light.

Light meals – the best type of evening meal.

Keep it small and simple if you can. Serve a salad, soup or fruit with bread and spreads. Some family members may disagree with the 'small evening meal' principle, especially if they have been out at work all day. Their views and needs should be respected!

This may sound like a radically different way of eating and cooking, and may even seem quite daunting at first. It may call for more preparation than do frozen dinners and other types of takeaways, but many healthy foods are very convenient themselves. Bananas are an example of a perfect convenience food!

It's worth investing in good equipment, like a steamer, for lightly cooking vegetables to conserve the maximum amount of their vitamins and minerals. Blenders save work and are helpful for many vegetarian recipes, and some come with coffee mill attachments, which are ideal for grinding nuts.

It takes time to get used to new ways of doing things, but it soon becomes easier. This is true of new ways of eating. The healthiest food is simple and easy to prepare. It is also delicious, with delicate, natural flavours. Be sure that you season your food adequately, especially at first. Many people find vegetables tasteless and they miss the taste of meat. Using herbs and gentle spices helps to overcome this problem. There are a great variety of plant foods to choose from, and you may well find that you end up eating and enjoying a much wider range of foods than you did before.

Menu plans

Day 1

Breakfast (Main meal)
Fresh fruit
Apple
Cereal
Shredded wheat with raisins, sliced bananas and soya milk
Bread
Rye crispbread with peanut butter, fruit or a savoury spread

Lunch/dinner (Main meal)
Starch
Baked potato
Raw vegetables
Grated carrot salad with alfalfa sprouts
Cooked vegetable
Broccoli
High-protein
Nut roast with tomato sauce

Supper (Light meal)
Fruit/vegetable
Tomato soup
Starch
Crispbread with a spread

Day 2

Breakfast (Main meal)
Fresh fruit
Orange, apple
Cereal
Oatmeal porridge with raisins and cashew cream
Bread
Wholewheat toast with cashew cream and fruit spread

Lunch/dinner (Main meal)
Starch
Brown rice
Raw vegetables
Green salad (lettuce, cucumber, and so on with dressing)
Cooked vegetable
Vegetable stew (onions, carrots, tomatoes and so on)
High-protein
Beans (in stew)

Supper (Light meal)
Fruit/vegetable
Fruit salad with fruit cream
Starch
Granola

To buy
Apples
Bananas
Soya milk
Potatoes
Tomatoes
Basil
Carrots
Onions
Cashews
Rice
Cucumber

Day 3

Breakfast (Main meal)
Fresh fruit
  Mango
Cereal
  Cooked millet with sliced banana and chopped nuts
Bread
  Mixed-grain bread with peanut butter and dried fruit spread

Lunch/dinner (Main meal)
Starch
  Pasta (wholewheat)
Raw vegetables
  Green salad and grated carrot
Cooked vegetable
  Tomato/onion/pepper in the sauce for the pasta
High-protein
  Beans or textured vegetable protein in the pasta sauce

Supper (Light meal)
Fruit/vegetable
  Tomato salad
Starch
  Wholewheat bread with hummus and olives

Day 4

Breakfast (Main meal)
Fresh fruit
  Pear
Cereal
  Packet cereal with stewed apple and blackcurrants
Bread
  Wholewheat bread with tahini and marmite or fruit spread

Lunch/dinner (Main meal)
Starch
  Steamed potatoes
Raw vegetables
  Tomato, onion, cucumber, lettuce, cress, and so on
Cooked vegetable
  Aubergine stew with onions, peppers, tomatoes and so on
High-protein
  Hummus with crispbread

Supper (Light meal)
Fruit/vegetable
  Baked apple with dates
Starch
  Mixed-grain toast with honey and tahini

Day 5

Breakfast (Main meal)
Fresh fruit
  Tomatoes (large serving, cooked or raw)
Starch
  Baked potatoes with baked beans
Bread
  Crispbread with mashed avocado

Lunch/dinner (Main meal)
Starch
  Rice
Raw vegetables
  Grated carrots and beetroot with watercress
Cooked vegetable
  Stir-cooked mixed vegetables with bean shoots
High-protein
  Tofu pieces with cashews added to stir-cooked vegetables

Supper (Light meal)
Fruit/vegetable
  Fresh fruit selection
Starch
  Bread and spread

Packed lunches can be just as nutritious as cooked meals. The easiest sort is the fruit or salad and sandwiches type. Thermos jugs are useful for soup and other hot foods in cold climates. Insulated boxes or icepacks are good for keeping things cool in hot climates or warm buildings. If packed lunches are needed every day, it's important to vary the menu.

Suggested sandwich fillings – hummus, tofu cottage cheese, bean spread or avocado, all of which can be spread thickly and used with all sorts of salad to make delicious, vitamin-rich sandwiches. Nut butters, tahini or sunflower butter can also be used with yeast extract, with or without salad. They can also be used with sweet spreads – honey, malt extract, fruit spreads, or dried fruits. One or two fresh fruits can be included, or some extra salad. For dessert, add some pieces of dried fruit and a few nuts, or some whole-food cookies.

Recipes

This is a small selection of recipes that are helpful for making a change to a whole plant food diet. They are all 100% cholesterol free; they contain nothing refined, and so are suitable for weight loss and cholesterol-lowering diets. They are easy to prepare, and are flexible, so you can vary them with added ingredients and seasonings according to your taste.

Nut or seed butters

Use a coffee mill to grind nuts or seeds as finely as possible. Very finely ground nuts will form a butter with their own oil to hold it together. Less finely ground nuts and seeds will need some extra liquid. Rather than extra oil, add just enough water to make a creamy paste. This will keep for up to a week in the fridge, so make it in small quantities. Any kind of nuts can be used. Peanuts, hazelnuts and cashews are particularly good if they are toasted first. Sesame and sunflower seeds can be used for butters, and mixtures of nuts or of nuts and seeds can also be used.

Fruit spread (whole-fruit jam)

For dried fruit spreads, soak or cook the fruit in a little water until it is fairly soft, then mash or blend to the consistency you like. Dates only need to be mashed; figs and apricots may be better if briefly blended. Dried fruit can be used to sweeten fresh fruit – for example, equal quantities of fresh or frozen blackcurrants and dates cooked together make a delicious spread.

Savoury spreads

Mash up well-cooked beans, and add plenty of your own choice of flavourings – garlic, tomato sauce, Marmite, herbs, olives, and so on. Use for sandwich fillings.

Tomato sauce

Gently cook together a chopped onion, a stick of celery and a small, sweet red or green pepper in a little water.* Add a medium-sized tin of chopped tomatoes or a half-kilo of peeled and chopped fresh tomatoes, 3 or 4 tablespoonfuls of tomato purée, and your choice of herbs and seasonings. Cook gently for an hour or so if you have time!

*It is good to avoid all oil if there are serious health problems, especially if there is a need to lose weight. However, virgin olive oil is not a refined product, and has health benefits as well as a pleasant flavour; a mixture of equal parts of olive oil and water can be used.**

Nut roast

This can be baked in a loaf tin and used as the high-protein part of a main meal. It can be made into burgers and baked, grilled (or even fried), and also used as a savoury pie filling. If a little more liquid is used, it can be baked in a casserole dish and used as a pâté to spread on toast or for sandwiches.

Blend together: 1 medium onion, 1 stick celery, 1 tablespoon yeast extract and 1 cup water. Add to 1 cup nuts (already ground), 2 cups wholemeal breadcrumbs and 1 tablespoon dried mixed herbs. Mix well and bake in a moderate oven until firm and golden brown on top.

Granola

Blend two ripe bananas, ½ cup honey or 1 cup date butter,* ½ cup tahini (sesame purée), and add to 6 cups porridge oats, 1 cup shredded coconut and 1 cup sunflower seeds. Mix thoroughly, spread on baking trays and cook slowly in a cool oven. When completely dry, store in an airtight tin.

*Date butter – briefly soak 1 cup dates in boiling water, then blend to a smooth paste.**

Flapjack

Mix together 1 cup whole peanut butter, 3 cups porridge oats, and ½ cup honey, with just enough water to bind it together. Spread smoothly on a baking tray and cook for 20-30 minutes until golden brown at 180°C.

Banana-date-nut cookies (BDN cookies)
No added fat and no added sugar – 100% nutritious!
- 3 bananas
- 1 cup chopped dates
- ½ cup chopped walnuts
- 1 cup raisins
- 1 cup shredded coconut
- 2 cups porridge oats

Mash the bananas and add the other ingredients. Stir well. Drop by spoonfuls on an oiled baking tray and bake at 180°C until golden brown.

Fruit cream
Take 1/2 cup cashew cream, 1 cup orange juice and 2 bananas. Blend well and serve with fruit salad, or with breakfast cereal.

Fruit smoothie
Blend a mixture of fruits and fruit juice, sweetening if necessary with honey or apple juice concentrate. Try orange juice with frozen bananas and dried apricots or strawberries. Experiment with different fruits, and add soya, coconut or cashew milk for a creamier texture. This can also be frozen to make a delicious fruit ice cream.

Standard citronette salad dressing
- ½ cup olive oil
- ¼ cup lemon juice
- 2 tablespoons yeast flakes
- 1 tablespoon garlic purée (or crushed fresh garlic to taste)
- 1 teaspoon herb salt or to taste

Put all the ingredients in a screw-topped jar, screw the lid on tightly and shake vigorously for a few seconds until emulsified. This keeps in the fridge for several weeks, and can be used for all kinds of salads. For smaller amounts use the same proportions of oil and lemon, adding the other ingredients to taste.

Oil-free salad dressing
Replace the oil with cashew or sunflower cream or soya milk, or a mixture of any of these.

Cashew milk and cream
Cook a cup of cashew nuts for a few minutes in just enough water to cover them. Let them cool for a few minutes, then blend on high speed until really smooth – at least one minute. This thick cream can be used as it is, or it can be diluted by adding one cup of water for 'single cream', or 3 cupfuls for 'milk'. This cream can be frozen. Other nuts can be used, but they do not make quite such a smooth cream as cashews.

6 We are what we eat

Countless thousands of research papers have established the firm connection between lifestyle and quality and length of life. The concept of whole-person health involves the interrelationship of all aspects of lifestyle – diet, exercise, substance use, stress levels and mental status. Optimum health includes the avoidance of all the major killer diseases.

Your body needs premium fuel

It would be difficult to overestimate the importance of diet in this. Choosing good food is a major part of choosing good health. Good food is one of the most important lifestyle factors that lead to health and longevity. For our food to have its optimum effect it needs to be part of a consistent lifestyle that includes vigorous exercise, the avoidance of poisons and a peaceful frame of mind. The high-fat, high-sugar diet of the Western countries, and its heavy dependence on animal products, is taking its toll. This, with the sedentary lifestyle and the use of poisons like alcohol, tobacco and caffeine, is why, although life expectancy is longer than ever, people in rich countries can expect to end their lives with ten or more years of chronic ill health. Degenerative diseases account for most of this suffering.

The degenerative diseases were known as the diseases of Western civilisation. In the past only the rich in most parts of Africa, India and Latin America needed to fear them, but now the increasing popularity of the Western lifestyle is adding its burden of degenerative diseases there too. They are difficult and expensive to treat, and even the most prosperous societies find it difficult to meet the demands of advancing medicine in the battle with degenerative disease. How can societies with poorly developed economies begin to cope with such a burden?

Prevention is better than cure

Fortunately, prevention is a great deal simpler and cheaper than any cure, and knowing the causes of the problems enables us to learn how to prevent and, often, even to reverse them, which is the real solution to the dilemma.

Poor nutrition is responsible for much of the world's misery and there is poor nutrition in every society. In the West the main problem is overnutrition: too much food of the wrong sort. Around the year 2000, according to EU statistics, the UK achieved the dubious distinction, which they still have more than a decade later, of being the most overweight nation in Europe, though still behind the US. This is in sharp contrast to the situation in many poor countries, where undernutrition is a major problem because they just don't have enough food to go around.

The obesity that results from overnutrition is not classed as a disease itself, but it is a very serious health problem, because it contributes to so many other diseases. Almost all the degenerative diseases are more common, occur earlier, are more difficult to treat and are more often fatal in the seriously overweight. That includes heart disease, stroke, cancer, diabetes, gall bladder problems, arthritis, varicose veins, eczema and almost any problem you care to name. Weight reduction is very desirable and it's a serious business, a multimillion-dollar industry in fact. However, many overweight people spend most of their lives on diets of one kind or another, but with little real or lasting benefit.

The ideal diet

Just as cars perform best when the maker's instructions are followed, so our bodies perform best when we obey the laws of health – the Maker's instructions, in fact. The story of the creation of the world, found at the beginning of the first book in the Bible, gives some interesting guidelines. Our earliest ancestors lived in a rural environment and had outdoor physical work and a plant food diet, and this is still the ideal situation for optimum health. This is worth keeping in mind, even if we live in a city and have a sedentary job. The principle is to do the best you can, whenever you can, while seeking the most natural surroundings available – parks, gardens, tree-lined streets – for brisk walks, or relaxing moments. Choose to eat the freshest and most natural plant foods that you can find – even growing some in window boxes or on balconies. And maintain the spiritual life with regular worship, praise and prayer.

A quick guide to nutrition

We need food for energy. It's the fuel our bodies burn to provide the energy for all our activities, and all our body's complex biochemical processes. Food energy is measured in calories. High-calorie food is high-energy food. This is just what you need if you are about to expend a lot of energy in strenuous manual work or sport, but it's not what you need if you spend most of your work and leisure sitting down in a warm and comfortable environment.

Food fuel comes in three different forms: **protein**, **carbohydrate** and **fat**. For optimum health we need each of these in the right proportions for our own particular needs, depending on our age, occupation, state of health, and the climate we live in.

The **nutritional** calorie – also known as the **dietary** or **food** calorie (symbol: Cal) – is used to measure the amount of energy that is required to raise the temperature of one kilogram of water by one degree Celsius. It may be spelt with a capital C at times and must be distinguished from the small or **gram** calorie (symbol: cal), which is used to measure the amount of energy needed to raise the temperature of one gram of water by one degree Celsius. Therefore, one Calorie (Cal) is equivalent to 1,000 calories (cal).

Proteins – the body-building foods

This is the building food, used for growth, repair and maintenance of body tissues, and also in the manufacture of all the hormones and enzymes that direct the body's complex chemical processes. Plant foods are good sources of protein. The most concentrated sources are the pulses – the peas, beans and lentils. Nuts and seeds are high in protein and fat, and grains average about ten percent protein by weight. Fruits and vegetables contain protein too, because it forms part of the structure of all plant cells. Protein-rich foods of animal origin are meat, fish, poultry, eggs and dairy products.

Our bodies are wonderfully designed machines, and if treated well they work very efficiently and economically. Much of the protein that is used for maintenance and repair is recycled, so we don't need a large intake and it's difficult to go short of protein unless you are actually short of food. Contrary to what nutritionists thought in the past, completely plant-food diets contain plenty of protein: meat eaters risk getting too much.

Proteins are complex molecules made up of long chains of **amino acids**, each protein having its own individual characteristic structure. The amino acids are made of carbon, hydrogen, oxygen and nitrogen. During digestion, the proteins are broken down to their component amino acids, which are then transported in the bloodstream to wherever they are needed for growth, repair, maintenance or manufacture. Any amino acids that are surplus to requirements are prepared for disposal – the nitrogen part is removed by the liver, and the kidneys send it out in the urine. This gives extra work for the liver, kidneys and also the heart. The remaining part of the amino acid is either used as fuel or converted to fat and stored for later use. When burnt as fuel in the body, one gram of protein produces four calories of energy.

We now know that animal protein as well as saturated animal fat contributes to high blood cholesterol levels. Plant proteins come without the baggage of cholesterol, saturated fat and other disease-related substances. Plant proteins come with fibre and other health-promoting substances. Plant protein is *superior*.

Three protein myths

'Human beings need lots of protein, the more the better' – so said Professor Karl Voigt, the great pioneer biochemist, who decided that the best way to discover the body's protein requirement was to observe how much protein healthy manual workers chose to eat. This led him to recommend 140g of protein per day for adult males. Only a few years later, Professor Chittenden did a scientific study in which he measured the amount of protein actually used in the body, and he discovered that only 42g per day were needed. His student volunteers tried the low-protein diet with great success, and he himself followed it for the rest of his life. Since that time many other physiologists have confirmed that low-protein diets are adequate, and over the years the recommended daily allowance has gradually dropped. The WHO now recommends that 50g a day is adequate for all adults, including pregnant and nursing mothers. It's now recognised that not only is lower protein adequate; it's better, as it is associated with a lower incidence of degenerative disease.

'Vegetarians lack protein' – not true. There is plenty of protein in plant foods. The starchy grains and vegetables that form the basis of healthy plant food diets are high enough in protein to supply most of what's needed. Pulses, nuts and seeds, and even fruits and vegetables, supply the rest. In fact, it would really need some careful thought to devise a plant food diet that was both interesting enough to eat and inadequate in protein. There really isn't any danger, if you choose a wide variety of foods from day to day to ensure a good supply of the different amino acids.

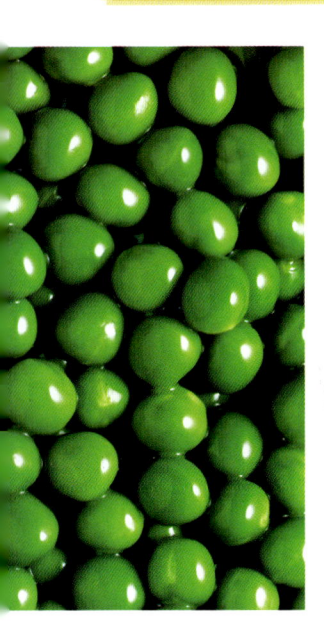

'Plant protein is inferior' – this is the old myth about first- and second-class proteins. Animal proteins were considered to be first-class or complete proteins, because the balance of amino acids in them was the most similar to the total balance in our own tissues. Plant proteins are more variable; some have more of one amino acid and less of another than human tissues do, so they were designated as second-class or incomplete proteins – and therefore less adequate. The fact is that our cells are able to pick and choose from the pool of amino acids in the bloodstream that results from the digestion of the different types of protein, and, as long as you eat a variety of plant proteins, you are not going to have any problems on a plant food diet.

Carbohydrates – the fuel foods

The name means that they are composed of carbon and water – no nitrogen here to stress the liver and kidneys – in fact, the ideal fuel. There are two main types, starches and sugars. They are all constructed from simple sugar units of six carbon atoms with hydrogen and oxygen.

The sugars

Sugar is a premium fuel and is the body's first choice for instant energy. It burns very easily and cleanly, producing energy (four calories per gram), carbon dioxide and water.

The best-known simple sugar molecule is **glucose** – widely advertised as a source of instant energy, and the main form in which sugar is transported in the blood. **Sucrose** is the most widely used sugar. It is formed from two simple sugar molecules (glucose and fructose) joined together. It's very easily broken down in the digestive tract, and absorbed almost as quickly as glucose. **Fructose** is the main sugar in fruit, very widely used as a sweetener as it is both sweeter and cheaper than sucrose. The best way to satisfy our sweet tooth is to eat it in its natural state in fruit. When it's removed and used as a sweetener, for example in biscuits or soft drinks, it is not a healthy food, as it is more easily converted to fat than other sugars.

Sugar problems

Simple sugars have the advantage of being very rapidly absorbed for emergency energy supplies, but if large amounts are eaten, they have the disadvantage that their rapid absorption can raise the blood sugar level too quickly. This can precipitate a reflex lowering of the blood sugar, causing it to fall too fast, with symptoms of weakness, shakiness or irritability and hunger. The slow absorption of the sugar molecules from the breakdown of the starches gives a much more long-lasting feeling of satisfaction after the meal, and maintains a much more stable blood sugar level. The ideal is to base the meals on the complex carbohydrates, add plenty of fruits or vegetables, and limit the use of refined sugar.

Simple sugars have more disadvantages. They are very harmful to the teeth, especially children's teeth, and especially if kept in frequent or prolonged contact with the teeth. Sweets and biscuits between meals, and the frequent use of sugary soft drinks, can cause major problems. Another harmful effect is that sugar decreases the ability of the white blood cells to fight infection. Then there's obesity. In the West most sugar is eaten in the refined form. It has lost all its vitamins, minerals and fibre. The sugar eater needs those missing nutrients, but interprets the dissatisfaction as a need for more sugar – more empty calories, worse nutrition – and where do the extra calories go? They are stored as fat, or worse still used to provide energy for restless, irritable behaviour.

The starches

Starches are long chains of simple sugar molecules linked together, each type of starch with its own characteristic pattern. These complex carbohydrate molecules take longer to break down in the digestive tract, and are absorbed much more slowly, giving a much longer feeling of satisfaction and maintaining a much more stable blood sugar level. Important sources of starches are all the grains and the starchy vegetables like potatoes and yams. The unrefined starches are best because they have their full complement of nutrients and fibre, such as wholewheat bread and brown rice.

The **glycaemic index**, or GI, is a measure of the effects of carbohydrate foods on blood sugar levels. It indicates how quickly the sugar they contain is absorbed into the bloodstream. Foods that are rapidly digested and absorbed – for example, high-sugar foods and snacks – have a high GI and can cause marked changes in blood sugar levels. Foods that are slowly digested and absorbed, such as wholewheat bread and brown rice, have a low GI and produce a stable blood sugar level. Low-GI foods have proven health benefits, especially for people with diabetes. They also help with weight control, because they are more satisfying: so helping to control appetite and delay hunger.

So how do we know what to eat? Working out the GI levels of one's diet could be as complex and tedious as counting calories, but this isn't necessary. There are some exceptions, but in general the refined carbohydrates – white bread, cakes, biscuits and so on – are the high-GI foods, and the whole, unrefined plant foods are the low-GI foods. The natural, unrefined plant food diet will have the lowest GI, and another piece of good news is that low-GI foods slow down the digestion of high-GI foods, so lowering the GI level of the whole meal.

Empty calories (junk food)

These are the calories, or food energy units, that come from refined sugar, fats and starches. They include white sugars, vegetable oil, white flour, and all foods made mainly from them. Confectionery is mainly sugar; soft drinks are sugared water. Cakes, biscuits and puddings are usually high in all three. Crisps and other savoury snacks are very high in fat, and also in salt. These foods provide very little more than fuel because they have lost their vital nutrients and fibre. Having lost all or most of their minerals and vitamins, they don't contribute much to health maintenance either. In addition, because they are so concentrated, they are not filling, and the temptation to overeat is hard to resist. They make a very major contribution to obesity and health problems of every kind.

Healthy and active people can usually cope with small amounts of junk food on an occasional basis, especially if they exercise vigorously to burn the calories up. If the junk food is a large part of the diet, there is a price to pay in ill health, present or future, or both.

Fats – the concentrated fuels

Fats are concentrated fuel sources, producing nine and a half calories of energy per gram – more than twice as much as carbohydrates or proteins. They are complex molecules, constructed from carbon, hydrogen and oxygen. After digestion they enter the bloodstream to be distributed for use as fuel. If fuel is not needed, they go to the fat storage cells. Fats are essential for good health, and, as there are traces of fats and oils in almost all foods, there is no danger of going short.

A simple guide to choosing fats

The different kinds of fats are classified according to the structure of their molecules.

Almost everybody has heard of saturated and unsaturated fats, if only from margarine tubs. This distinction has become very important to the food industry because the saturated fats are associated with raised levels of blood cholesterol, which in turn is linked to increased risk of heart attack and stroke. This has led to the development of a whole industry producing 'low-fat spreads' and other reduced-fat foods in the hope that they will help to prevent heart disease.

You don't need to be a biochemist or food scientist to choose the right food for your heart. All edible fats are mixtures of the different kinds of fat, but usually one predominates and gives that fat its particular properties. The more saturated the fat, the higher its melting point, which means that saturated fats are solid at room temperatures and unsaturated fats are liquid at room temperatures. Animals produce mainly saturated fats in their bodies – examples are butter, lard, and the fat of bacon and red meat – all of them solid at normal room temperature. Plants, with the two notable exceptions of coconut and palm, produce mainly unsaturated fats – oils that are liquid at room temperatures, and even in the fridge. They can be solidified by the process of hydrogenation, which turns them into saturated fats, which are more convenient for some purposes, but less healthy.

Disadvantages of vegetable oils

As heart disease is associated with saturated fat, and saturated fat is mainly of animal origin, vegetable fat is a better choice. However, vegetable oils are usually highly refined and processed. Typical sources are soybeans, corn and sunflower seeds. To make one tablespoonful of corn oil takes many more corn cobs than any normal person would eat at a sitting, but most people could very easily consume several spoonfuls of corn oil if it was in the form of margarine or mayonnaise, or hidden in biscuits or pastry. As well as making it easy to overconsume, the refining process has removed many vital nutrients, leaving a concentrated but deficient food.

The dreaded trans fats

Not only are these refined fats deficient, but they are easily damaged by very high temperatures in industrial processes. The structure of their molecules is changed in a way that contributes to tissue damage, ageing and cancer. These are the trans fats, which increase when the oils are cooked at high temperatures, as in frying. The reheating of oils in deep fryers compounds the problem. Limit the use of vegetable oils if you are fit and healthy. Avoid them if you are overweight or have health problems.

Olive oil is rather different. For a start, it need not be refined. The cold-pressed virgin olive oil is a completely natural product, comprising about 16% of the olive. What has been discarded is mainly fibre. The oil contains health-promoting phytochemicals, and its use as the main dietary fat is associated with low levels of heart disease. It's an important part of the Mediterranean diet, with its reduced levels of heart disease and cancer. Its main component is monounsaturated fat – halfway between the poly-unsaturated and the saturated fats. Olive oil seems to be the safest form of added fat (fat that is added to food, rather than being a natural part of it).

Fat adds interest and texture to food, and also helps to give a feeling of satisfaction. The best way to eat fat is as it occurs naturally in the different types of whole plant food. Some of these, like nuts and seeds, have a high fat content. Avocados, like olives, are loaded with fat, but it is a healthy type, and few, if any, need to cut these delicious plant foods out of their diet, unless they have specific problems with digesting them.

Progress in medicine and nutritional science doesn't happen along a straight line. New ideas tend to be accepted either overenthusiastically or not at all. This has been the case with fats. Some doctors and nutritionists went to the extreme of condemning all fat. The food industry took this up with lots of low-fat foods. In many low-fat cakes and biscuits the fat is replaced by sugar. Because the low-fat versions are not so satisfying, more is eaten, and the net result of the low-fat foods is that people gain even more weight.

What is one to do? The secret is to avoid processed foods and eat simple, natural, unrefined foods. It is almost impossible to overeat unprocessed plant foods with all their fibre intact, and with their own naturally occurring fat, rather than added fat. Such food has the added benefit of improving health and helping to prevent disease. Go for the simple, natural, unrefined plant foods and enjoy your food without worrying about the complicated chemistry of dietary fat.

Phytochemicals

These are being named 'the vitamins of the twenty-first century'. They are chemicals that are only found in plants: plant chemicals, compounds that give plants their special characteristics including taste, smell, colour, and healing properties. In the last few years many phytochemicals have been discovered to have anti-cancer properties, and some examples of these are the Brassica family – cabbage, broccoli, Brussels sprouts, and so on; the carrot family, which includes celery, parsnips, parsley and coriander; and the onion and garlic family. They occur in fruits and grains as well, and every plant food that has been studied so far contains valuable health-promoting phytochemicals.

Fibre is the indigestible residue of plant foods. All plant foods in their natural state contain fibre, because it is an important part of plant structure. Unrefined cereal grains are a good source. Most of their fibre is in the outer layer of bran, which is removed in the refining process. Fruits and vegetables, pulses, nuts and seeds all contain fibre. Animal produce does not contain any dietary fibre at all. White flour and rice have lost much of their fibre. Sugar and vegetable oils have lost it all.

Fibre has two very important functions – **filler** and **mover**. As filler, it gives bulk to the food, and gives a feeling of fullness, which is lacking when refined food is eaten. This feeling of fullness helps us to know when to stop eating, and lack of fibre is one of the main reasons for overweight. This is why natural, high-fibre food is an essential part of any successful weight-watching programme, and why it plays an important part in the prevention of many diseases.

As mover, the fibre bulk enables the whole digestive tract to work more easily. The bulky material also retains fluid, and this helps the colon to pass it through quickly, preventing constipation and all its associated problems, from piles to bowel cancer.

There is an added bonus with the soluble fibre in oats, fruits and vegetables – it also acts as a cholesterol trap, moving it right out of the system with the rest of the waste.

Water

Fruits and vegetables in their fresh and natural state have a high water content. This is by design, and its function is to give a sense of fullness and satisfaction after eating them, and also to help maintain our water input. Another of the problems with refined foods is that, as well as lacking fibre, they also lack water. This makes them even more concentrated, and less filling.

Water intake is very important. Recommendations vary from one to two litres a day: more in hot weather, or when exercising strenuously. Good hydration has many bonuses. It boosts the immune system, so helping to resist infections. It thins the blood, lowering the blood pressure and helping to prevent heart attacks, strokes and blood clots. It also helps to relieve headaches and many muscular aches and pains. A good rule of thumb is to drink enough to keep the urine pale and clear. In practical terms this will work out to six to eight glasses a day for most people. One regime is to start the day with a large drink of water on rising, say a pint (a generous half-litre), and then take mid-morning, mid-afternoon and mid-evening drinks. It is better not to drink very much with meals, as the fluids dilute the digestive juices, and slow down the digestive process.

Cooking to conserve vitamins and minerals

Food minerals are soluble in water and are easily lost if foods are cooked in water and the water is thrown away. To avoid this they should be cooked in as little water as possible and the water should also be used. Steaming is a good method, especially if the water is saved and used for gravy or soup, or simply drunk. Stews and soups conserve all the minerals, as do methods of baking and roasting whole vegetables (and fruits).

Water-soluble vitamins are also lost if cooking water is discarded, but they are also destroyed by heat, especially overcooking. Quick cooking, starting with the water already boiling, or the oven already hot, minimises the vitamin loss due to heat. Slow cooking, starting from cold and gradually warming up, gives enzymes plenty of time to destroy them.

Raw fruits and vegetables obviously contain the most vitamins and minerals, and it is a good plan to eat something raw at every meal. It is not necessary to eat all the fruits and vegetables raw, however, as some nutrients are more available when the food is cooked.

Other nutrients – vitamins and minerals

Vitamins are complex organic substances present in tiny quantities in food and essential for normal body function and maintenance.

They come in two varieties: fat-soluble (A, D, E and K) and water-soluble (B and C).

The fat-soluble ones come with fats and oils in food. They are absorbed along with dietary fat, which is another reason to avoid unnaturally low-fat diets.

The fat-soluble vitamins are stored in the liver and fat tissues, and this fact makes it possible to get too much if you take too many vitamin supplements.

Fat-soluble vitamins

Vitamin A works like a hormone, and has roles in vision, skin, lungs, bones, reproduction and more. Deficiency causes blindness, sickness and death, and is a major problem in many parts of the world. Animal food sources are milk, eggs and liver. In plant foods it comes in the form of beta carotene, which is changed to vitamin A in the body. It is a bright orange colour, and it comes in bright orange, yellow and green vegetables and fruits, such as carrots, greens and apricots. Beta carotene is also a powerful antioxidant (see box).

Antioxidants and free radicals

As the body's cells use oxygen to produce energy, some highly unstable molecules known as free radicals are produced. These are atoms or molecules with missing electrons. They rush around grabbing electrons from other molecules to stabilise themselves, in the process creating new free radicals. An electron-grabbing chain reaction starts that damages tissues and contributes to ageing and degenerative disease. The 'police' who put a stop to this are the antioxidants, among which are vitamins E, C and beta carotene. Many phytochemicals are also powerful antioxidants – for example, lycopene, the red pigment in tomatoes, strawberries and other red fruits, and resveratrol, the red pigment in grape skins. They seek out the free radicals and inactivate them – becoming inactivated themselves in the process. For this reason a regular supply of antioxidants is needed, and the best way of ensuring this is (of course) to eat a natural, unrefined plant food diet.

Vitamin D occurs in fish oils and eggs, and is added to margarine – but it is also synthesised in the skin when it is exposed to sunlight. Vitamin D was thought to be mainly concerned with bones and minerals, as deficiency causes rickets in children and bone degeneration in adults. More recently, it has been found to be involved in many health-promoting processes, including the prevention of heart disease and cancer. It is toxic in excess.

Vitamin E works to preserve cell membranes, especially in the lungs and blood cells. It is also a powerful antioxidant. It is found in many plant foods, particularly oils, and also in fruits and vegetables. Animal sources of small amounts are meat, fish and eggs. Deficiency and toxicity are both rare.

Vitamin K is one of the twenty-eight or more factors involved in blood clotting. It is found in greens and beans, and in milk and eggs. About half our supply of this vitamin is manufactured in our bodies by bacteria in our digestive tracts. Deficiency, which is rare, causes problems with bleeding. Excess, usually due to unwise supplementation, is also rare, and is toxic.

Water-soluble vitamins

Vitamin B complex. Vitamin B is not a single substance, but a group of over a dozen, which work together to facilitate the work of every cell – in every system, including the nervous system. Some are involved in generating energy, some in the manufacture of proteins and new cells. They are essential for the metabolism of carbohydrates, fats and proteins, and deficiency leads to serious diseases. They are abundantly supplied in natural, unprocessed foods, both plant and animal. The outer layers of grains are a rich source, and serious deficiency diseases occurred when the refining of wheat and other grains became common practice. Some of the lost B complex vitamins are now added to white flour to avoid this problem. Milder deficiencies contribute to irritability and nervous tension. Other plant sources are beans and green vegetables. Nutritional yeast and yeast extract are particularly rich sources.

Vitamin B12 is rather special and mysterious. It is manufactured by bacteria and it occurs in animal produce. It is not made by plants, nor can our bodies synthesise it. This has led to the belief that animal products are essential. However, many total vegetarians (vegans) survive very well for many years without either animal foods or B12 supplements. Where do they get their B12? Bacteria produce it, and bacteria are working away in all sorts of unexpected places. Also, vitamin B12 is added to some commonly used foods, such as soya milk, breakfast cereals and yeast extract. We only need very minute amounts, and most vegans probably get enough, though some will need to take supplements. Problems occur, even in meat eaters, when vitamin B12 can't be absorbed. The onset of these problems, which include pernicious anaemia and degeneration of the spinal cord, is very gradual as B12 is stored in the body, and most people have about a four-year reserve. As these illnesses are very serious, it's recommended that people changing to totally vegetarian diets, especially in later life, have occasional B12 blood tests, just to make sure that they are absorbing the very tiny amounts that occur in their exclusively plant-food diets.

Vitamin C has been known longer than any other vitamin. Hundreds of years ago sailors on long voyages suffered from scurvy, due to lack of vitamin C, until it was discovered that adding citrus fruit or cabbage (both good sources of vitamin C) cured them. It is another antioxidant. It maintains connective tissue, speeds up the healing of wounds, protects against infection and promotes iron absorption, among many other functions. Its antioxidant properties help to slow down the ageing process and the development of all the degenerative diseases. It is found in all fresh fruits and vegetables, but it is destroyed by heat, and once the produce has been picked, the content gradually diminishes.

Major minerals are calcium, phosphorus, potassium, sodium, chlorine and iron. Plant foods contain all the minerals we need, and in the right combinations; however, large amounts of them can be lost in cooking. See box on page 73.

Calcium is used for building bones and teeth, and also has roles in nerve transmission, muscle contraction, blood clotting and other important functions. Its most well-known source is dairy produce, but what is less well-known is that the calcium in dairy produce is not in the most easily absorbed form. Calcium is also widely distributed in plant foods like green vegetables, grains, nuts and seeds, mostly in an easily absorbed form. Deficiency causes rickets in children and bone degeneration in adults.

Phosphorus is also important in bones and teeth, and in cell membranes and genetic material. It has vital functions in maintaining acid-base balance and in energy production. It is highest in animal produce, but is present in many plants, and deficiency is unlikely on almost any diet.

Magnesium is necessary for the operation of hundreds of enzymes. Good sources are beans, potatoes, spinach and sunflower seeds. Deficiency has been linked to heart disease, chronic fatigue and many other illnesses.

Sodium. No known human diet lacks this element, which has many important functions in maintaining the body fluids, and therefore the function of every organ and tissue. Excess is a common result of eating too much salt. Savoury snacks and many processed foods are very high in salt. Animal produce is also high in sodium. High sodium intake is associated with high blood pressure, heart attack, stroke and some cancers. To eat a whole plant food diet with lots of fruit is a good way to reduce salt intake to the small amount that we actually need.

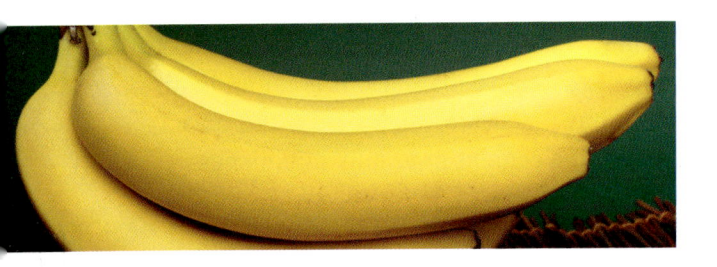

Potassium is very important inside the cells. It has many metabolic functions, including control of the action of the heart. Fresh fruits and vegetables are the best source. Deficiency is possible in some illnesses and with the use of some diuretic medicines. Supplements can cause excess, which is dangerous too.

Trace minerals: iodine, zinc, selenium, fluoride, chromium, copper and other minerals (including boron, nickel, manganese, silicon and molybdenum) are needed in very tiny amounts. Iodine is well-known for its relation to the thyroid gland. Zinc and selenium have multiple functions that involve the immune system and antioxidant activities, making them important factors in preventing cancer and other degenerative diseases. Most of these trace minerals are widely available in unrefined plant foods. Heavy use of refined foods makes deficiencies possible, with important effects in all the body systems. All the trace minerals are toxic in excess. Overuse of supplements is dangerous, underlining the fact that the safest way to get your minerals is from your food.

Iron is best known for its part in the structure of haemoglobin, the oxygen-carrying pigment in the red blood cells. Iron-deficiency anaemia is a worldwide problem. Diseases that cause blood loss are a major factor. Another one is inadequate iron in the diet, which often simply means inadequate food. Most people think that red meat is the most important source of iron, but although plant sources may contain less iron it is usually in a more easily-absorbed form. The richest plant sources are the dark-coloured ones – dark-green vegetables, beetroot, prunes, raisins and the dark outer layers of grains.

E-numbers and other additives

'E-numbers' refers to food additives permitted in the EU. Their use is a controversial subject. Some scientists reassure us that the additives are perfectly safe at the levels used; others quote research that shows the opposite. The best plan is to avoid artificial additives as far as possible. This can be done by choosing a simple, natural diet using large amounts of fresh fruits and vegetables, some of them raw, and using simple, natural home-made dishes rather than prepacked ones. If this is our regular diet, we can be sure that our livers will be in the best possible condition to deal with whatever artificial additives and pollutants we may accidentally or occasionally choose to eat.

Going organic: is it worth it?

This also used to be controversial, with conflicting evidence, but the balance of evidence is now in favour of these methods of agriculture that use organic fertilisers and avoid chemical pesticides. This is especially true with the introduction of genetically engineered food, one purpose of which seems to be to enable more pesticides to be used.

When we don't know the results of these types of interference with nature, it seems sensible to eat the simplest and most natural diet that is available. The ideal would be to grow our own food and eat it when it's at its freshest and best. Failing that, we should eat a wide variety of the freshest and most natural food we can afford, remembering that balance is what is important. Do the best that you can, praise God for the food on your plate, ask for His blessing as you eat it, and eat with a thankful heart.

7 Plant food is best

There has been a revolution in thinking about this subject in the last few years. The received opinion used to be that human beings needed to eat meat in order to preserve life, health and strength. This view was strengthened by the theory of evolution with its ideas of 'nature red in tooth and claw', and the idea that man had only fairly recently (in evolutionary terms) evolved from his carnivorous ancestors. Pictures of primitive cavemen gnawing on bones reinforced the idea. Some have even gone so far as to say that we have too recently evolved from our carnivorous past to be able to fully cope with complex carbohydrates. This, they say, explains the prevalence of wheat sensitivities. They completely overlook the fact that our carnivorous 'cousins' (cats and dogs are the most familiar examples) have completely different teeth, jaws and digestive systems in order to cope with meat, not to mention the many other major differences between human beings and their nearest animal 'relatives'. Nor did they know that archaeologists would find that the cave dwellers' diet included many plant foods as well as animal flesh, suggesting that these 'primitive' people had a mixed diet, and were hunter-gatherers, rather than just hunters.

The vegetarian: a new image

It's only a few decades since doctors and scientists questioned the adequacy of the vegetarian diet. The popular image of the vegetarian was of a pale, thin person, as opposed to the strong, healthy meat eater typified by the sturdy, hale-and-hearty farmer. The facts that the farmer's ruddy complexion owed much more to fresh air and exercise than to his diet, and that many farmers died in the prime of their lives from cardiovascular disease, were not appreciated. Today the healthy-looking vegetarian, who is usually enthusiastic for the other aspects of a healthy lifestyle as well, including exercise, has helped to change the old stereotypical image.

Back in the 1980s research by the National Advisory Committee on Nutrition Education revealed that people in the UK were overconsuming fat, sugar and red meat and would benefit from reducing these things and consuming more starches, fruit and vegetables. This was confirmed by the World Health Organisation in 1990. Since then we have learned about the phytochemicals in plant foods – substances with specific disease-preventing properties which are found only in plant foods. Plant food diets contain less total fat, less saturated fat, less salt, more fibre and many more phytochemicals. Plant food diets win whichever way you look at them!

Human beings are much more similar in anatomy and physiology to monkeys and apes than to carnivorous or herbivorous animals. Most primates are vegetarians most of the time, only eating meat when their preferred diet of plant food is out of season. Mainly plant food eaters, they are able to cope with meat if necessary. Human beings are similar in that they can cope with meat too; though, as scientists are now demonstrating, they don't do so well on it. 'We're basically a vegetarian species and should be eating a wide variety of plant foods and minimising our intake of animal foods.' So says Dr T. Colin Campbell of the China Study.

Even completely herbivorous animals can adapt, at least in the laboratory, to eating meat, and may even grow bigger, fatter and stronger, but unfortunately they are likely to collapse in their prime with fatal heart attacks.

Who lives longest?

There are few human groups that survive on an entirely animal food diet. The Eskimos were one example, living in a very cold climate on a very high-fat-and-protein fish diet. They were not noted for longevity, and when sugar was added to their diet the effect was disastrous: tooth decay, diabetes, cardiovascular disease and more, in epidemic proportions. The Masai in East Africa are another example that's often quoted. They live very active outdoor lives herding cattle, which provide them with their unique diet of milk and blood. In both cases survival of the fittest no doubt has played an important part.

Three groups particularly noted for their longevity in the past were the Hunza in northern Pakistan, the Vilcabamba in Ecuador and the Georgians in the Caucasus. Although their ages have been exaggerated at times, these groups did in the past have a much higher than average number of healthy and active elderly members. They all ate very largely plant food diets and lived in remote mountainous areas where a lot of vigorous physical activity was needed just to get around.

More recently the National Geographic Association have brought attention to the 'blue zones', areas where people are noted for their unusually long and healthy lives. The first three areas they looked at were the Japanese island of Okinawa, the Mediterranean island of Sardinia, and the town of Loma Linda in California. These groups, though in very different environments, all share these factors:

strong family and social support, energetic exercise habits, and a simple diet based on unrefined plant foods that enables them to maintain a healthy weight. The Loma Linda group are particularly remarkable because they don't live in a remote unpolluted rural area, but in semi-urban Southern California, and in this group most avoid flesh foods altogether.

Though diet is an important factor in 'blue zone' longevity, it's clearly not the only one.

For those living the comfortable Western lifestyle, in a less-than-ideal urban environment, meat eating is definitely not worth the increased risks of cardiovascular disease, cancer and other degenerative diseases. Loma Linda's Adventist health study showed that vegetarians had an advantage over meat eaters, where cancer and heart disease were concerned. The meat eaters were considerably more likely to have a heart attack or to develop cancer than the vegetarians, and the small group of strict vegetarians/vegans were the least at risk. Many thousands of research papers, from a vast range of different institutions, show similar results: meat eating is associated with a higher incidence of life-shortening heart disease and cancer. Processed meats, such as ham and bacon, are particularly associated with a higher incidence of cancer. Increased risks of many other degenerative diseases have also been noted, including gallstones, kidney stones, diverticulitis, arthritis and osteoporosis.

At risk

Meat eaters are also much more at risk from food poisoning, especially the dreaded salmonella. Food-borne infections are usually associated with animal produce: not only meat and poultry, but also dairy products and eggs. Mayonnaise, custard and creamed chicken are almost perfect culture media and we should treat them with care, especially in warm climates. Raw meat and poultry are potential carriers of infections such as salmonella, some strains of which are potentially very serious, and can be fatal. These foods need to be treated with great care and kept quite separate from salads and other foods that are not going to be cooked. Most of the regulations concerning kitchen hygiene and safety are about preventing the spread of infection from meat and poultry. Nor are dairy products and eggs free from problems. Eggs are notorious for their ability to spread salmonella, and the UK Food Standards Agency advises great care in handling eggs, and advises that raw egg should not be eaten at all. In commercial cooking pasteurised liquid egg is advised for lightly cooked egg recipes. Public health authorities also warn against soft cheeses made with unpasteurised milk, especially for pregnant mothers. Plant foods present problems if they have been contaminated by infected animal products, and outbreaks of food poisoning have even been traced to vegetables contaminated by infected manure and irrigation water. In tropical climates where bacteria multiply more quickly, and hygiene may be more difficult, it's important that everything that is going to be eaten raw is thoroughly washed.

Cholesterol

Then there is the question of cholesterol. Meat, poultry, fish, dairy produce and eggs *all* contain cholesterol, which everyone now knows is associated with an increased risk of cardiovascular disease. Saturated fat pushes the level of cholesterol even higher, and animal foods tend to be high in saturated fats. And don't be deceived about the low-fat varieties. They are not good, only less bad.

Meat lacks fibre

Another negative thing about animal produce is that it contains none of that healthy fibre that prevents constipation, reduces cholesterol levels and helps to prevent many diseases, from piles and irritable bowel syndrome to diverticulitis and bowel cancer. Plant fibre also gives a sense of satisfaction that prevents overeating and makes weight control easier. This is why, contrary to what used to be thought, vegetarians can lose weight more easily than meat eaters – if they choose whole plant foods.

Free radical alert

Animal products produce more free radicals, the 'wild' atoms and molecules that race around and damage cell membranes, contributing to ageing, heart disease and cancer. Plant foods contain the 'trouble-shooting' antioxidants that inactivate them. It's not necessary to study a course in nutrition to deduce that plant foods are preferable to animal foods where prevention of degenerative disease is concerned.

The animal welfare argument

In the UK alone, 800 million animals are slaughtered for food each year. This of course includes birds as well as large farm animals. They are all sentient creatures, capable of feeling pain and pleasure, fear and contentment. Some of them are more intelligent than many of our domestic pets. They were created for our pleasure and service, not for us to exploit and torture, keeping them in unnatural surroundings, feeding them unnatural food, denying them the satisfaction of their most basic instincts. Raising poultry in battery cages is the most obvious, but there are many other cruel practices where animals are considered merely as meat machines, bred to exploit the characteristics that are the most financially rewarding, with little thought for the animal's comfort or health. Many people are vegetarians because they want to have no part in this industry. Nor is the dairy industry exempt, and vegans with their completely plant food diets have often chosen this way of life and eating out of respect for the animals and the desire to live in harmony with nature and the environment.

Environmental issues

Environmental and economic issues also favour a plant food diet. To produce meat as a staple food is an economic disaster. It takes ten times as much land to produce a pound of red meat as it does a pound of grain. Fifty per cent of the world cereal production is used as animal feed. It's not too difficult to calculate that the world could quite easily produce food for several times its present vast population if only plant foods were used. According to the FAO (Food and Agriculture Organisation of the United Nations) animal husbandry poses many serious threats to the environment: it's a major source of greenhouse gases worldwide and it's the leading source of water pollution. The methane produced by cattle contributes to the greenhouse effect, and the ammonia from animal waste joins with that from fertilisers to produce the acid rain that damages trees and buildings.

Animal husbandry is also responsible for land degradation – erosion and other damage to the land itself – and for loss of biodiversity (it reduces the range of plant and animal species). Meat production, with its heavy dependence on artificial fertilisers and chemicals for pest control, is actually damaging our environment beyond repair. Overfishing has depleted the seas and intensive grazing erodes the land. Choosing a plant food diet is one of the most important contributions one can make to preserving the environment.

Meat eating is becoming less popular in many parts of the world, particularly in the UK, where the numbers of vegetarians and vegans are growing. Definitions of 'vegetarian' vary, as some would include only those who never eat meat, poultry or fish, while others would include those who very occasionally eat some of those things. There are a great many 'nearly vegetarians' and also 'meat reducers', who have several meat-free days each week.

Re-educating the tastebuds

The only reasonable answer to the question, 'Why eat meat?' must be, 'Because I like it.' Here is where many make a mistake. They like meat, and are disappointed that vegetarian food cannot duplicate its flavour. They sacrifice their health because they don't realise that plant foods have wonderful flavours of their own, and that taste buds are flexible. It takes a few weeks, or at most a few months, to re-educate our taste buds. For example, soya milk may taste quite awful the first time it's tried. After all, it tastes nothing like cows' milk. However, most people who stick to soya milk, and don't keep reminding themselves of the taste of cows' milk, will before long find that soya is tolerable, and will eventually come to prefer it, especially if it is freeing them from some of the many unpleasant symptoms of cows' milk sensitivity. The solution is to decide what is best for your health, eat accordingly and be patient with your taste buds. Concentrate on enjoying new and different interesting tastes, and never look back as you eat for health, and not for taste alone.

The mind and the spirit

Physical health is not the only reason for choosing a plant food diet. The mind and spirit benefit as well. The Bible teaches that the Creator chose a plant food diet for His first children, Adam and Eve. Their work was to care for their garden home, and the animals were to be their companions, not their diet. Joy and peace are two of the rewards for choosing to eat according to the Creator's original plan.

Eating for health

Choose whole foods and solve your nutrition problems!

For optimum health, very nearly all our food should contain its full quota of nutrients. This means it should be whole and unrefined. This will ensure that you get enough fibre, as well as all the vitamins, minerals and phytochemicals that you need.

The importance of fibre

Fibre keeps the bowels functioning regularly, and prevents constipation and related problems, such as diverticulitis, and even bowel cancer. Fibre helps remove cholesterol from the body. Perhaps most important of all, it is bulky, filling the stomach and giving a sense of satisfaction that prevents overeating and excess weight gain.

Which foods have fibre?
All the whole plant foods contain some fibre, but the starchy grains are the main source: wheat, rice, barley, rye and so on. Beans and lentils, fruits and vegetables, nuts and seeds are other sources.

How much fibre is needed?
Make the starchy filler foods like grains and potatoes the basis of the diet. Then eat as much as you need to feel satisfied, while still leaving room for plenty of fruits or vegetables, and some of the concentrated higher-protein beans, lentils, nuts or seeds. This will ensure that you get all the fibre you need. You really can't go short of fibre on a whole plant food diet.

WARNING!
It's very possible to overdo the fibre if you add bran to your food. Instead, get the bran in its natural state as it comes as part of the whole grain: for example, in wholewheat bread, brown rice, and oat porridge.

Why *plant* foods for vitamins, minerals and phytochemicals?

Of course animal products contain vitamins and minerals, too, but no vitamin C and no phytochemicals. These are particularly important for building a strong immune system and helping to ward off diseases ranging from simple coughs and colds to heart disease and cancer.

Choosing a whole plant food diet means that you will automatically be eating less fat. The average person in the UK gets about 40% of his total calorie intake from fat. (Weight for weight, fat contains more than twice the calories of protein or carbohydrate.) If you eat whole plant foods, there is no problem with excess fat. You get the fat in its natural state, in the right amount, and with all the other nutrients in the right amount too. If you add a few nuts and seeds, or avocados and olives, to your grains, fruits and vegetable foods, you will get the healthy fat you need without having to worry about the unhealthy kind.

A note about oil

There are basically two kinds of vegetable oil. There is olive oil, which is around 16% of the olive and doesn't need to go through any refining process. It is rich in the monounsaturated fatty acids associated with healthy hearts and low blood pressure. Then there are all the other vegetable oils, which are usually highly refined. For example, it takes about twelve corncobs to get a tablespoonful of corn oil. All the fibre, protein and carbohydrate has been lost in the refining process, along with almost all the other nutrients, making it a very concentrated food and very easy to overeat.

Choosing whole plant foods means you will also automatically be eating less sugar. White sugar is a pure energy source, containing no nutrients whatsoever except calories. The average person in the UK gets 20% of his calories from sugar. It takes about a yard of sugarcane to make a teaspoonful of sugar – it's very easy to eat too much sugar, but impossible to overeat on sugarcane! Sugar is associated with all sorts of problems, from tooth decay to diabetes, but the real problem is the fact that it supplies empty calories – it is deficient in all the valuable nutrients that are lost in the refining process.

WARNING: Don't get the dangers of refined foods out of proportion

It is when they form a large part of the diet that they are so harmful. Small amounts occasionally are unlikely to be harmful to healthy, active people. Animal produce is a different problem. Now that there is so much disease in animals it would be wise to gradually give up the use of animal flesh altogether, and to be very careful about the other animal products as well.

What about plant protein?

It is completely adequate, provided you choose a variety of whole plant foods, including grains and pulses. Plant foods enable you to avoid the excess protein in meat, fish and poultry, and the stress it puts on your heart, liver and kidneys.

Making the transition

Unless there are urgent health reasons, make changes in your diet gradually – for some it can be done in a few weeks; others need several months, or even one or two years. The first step is to choose more whole foods, making a gradual change – for example, from white to wholewheat bread. Then start choosing bigger servings of vegetables and other whole plant foods, and choose smaller servings of the animal foods, gradually replacing them with a wide variety of plant foods. Be very careful about making major changes in diet if you live in a place where a wide variety of plant foods are not available. Take local advice about dairy produce and eggs. It's important that there is a good variety of different kinds of plant foods to take their place if they have been an important part of the diet.

Change challenge

In some places, for example the UK, it is easy to change to a vegetarian diet. Supermarkets offer an abundant variety of vegetables: fresh, frozen, tinned or preserved in other ways. Wholewheat bread and breakfast cereals are easy to find, as is wholewheat flour, and a variety of beans, lentils, nuts and even seeds. The frozen food cabinets hold a range of meat substitutes, ready to serve or cook, in attractive packages. What the supermarkets don't supply can be found in the health food shops. The new vegetarian should have no problem about getting enough variety.

Would-be vegetarians who live in countries where the food industry is less developed may feel that vegetarianism is just too difficult an option. But actually, many people living in countries with developed market economies envy those living in tropical countries who have access to outdoor market stalls where there is an abundant variety of fresh fruit and vegetables, along with beans, lentils, nuts and seeds, all in their natural state, free from the preservatives and additives used by the modern food industry.

Something better

Making changes in one's diet is much easier for some than for others. Some countries have an abundant variety of inexpensive wholesome plant foods in every large supermarket, but in smaller shops in isolated areas there may be much less choice, and more thoughtful planning is needed. In countries where vegetarians are less well-known and less well catered for it is different again. The fact is that living healthily does take more thought and care, at least in the beginning while you are getting used to it. Ready-made vegetarian dishes are convenient and save time, but are expensive, and are often high in fat and therefore not the most healthy. Such manufactured foods are by no means essential. It is possible to develop a healthy vegetarian diet anywhere there is a variety of fruits, vegetables and pulses (beans and lentils) and a supply of unrefined cereal products such as wholewheat bread, or locally used ethnic or regional cereals. Special vegetarian products are not necessary; nor are nuts, though they are nice if you can get them. Most ethnic diets are fairly easy to adapt as they are based around starchy foods. The secret is to make the changes gradually. For example, gradually increase the amount of vegetables, beans and so on as you reduce the amount of meat in the dishes, until finally they become vegetarian dishes. Be sure to use plenty of seasonings in the beginning to help get used to the meat-free taste.

Another real difficulty is when the rest of the household insist on meat. Making special vegetarian dishes can be just too much when you are very busy, and if you are not the cook it may be even worse, because the cook may be very unwilling to even try to prepare such food, and you probably don't want to impose that extra work on someone else either. So it's good to approach the subject of improving one's diet calmly and unhurriedly. The stress caused by the extra work could undo the benefit of the healthier food. 'Something better' is the watchword of all true food reform, and reform is progressive – you don't learn it all at once or make all the changes at the same time. You do the best you can as you gradually move towards what you decide is the best for yourself and your family.

8 Weight management

Obesity and its consequences

Obesity or overweight is the condition where excessive fat is stored in the body tissues. It is by far the most common form of malnutrition in the rich industrialised countries, but it is becoming a worldwide problem. The World Health Organisation describes it as an epidemic. It is a serious problem because it predisposes to a vast range of diseases. It is one of the major medical problems in the developed countries today, and it is also a problem wherever the sedentary, high-sugar and high-fat Western lifestyle is followed. Not only does excess weight reduce the efficiency of those affected and prevent them from enjoying many normal activities, but it is associated with a much higher incidence of many diseases and an appreciably higher death rate.

Some of these diseases, for example hernias and varicose veins, are simply due to the extra volume of fat itself. Some, like osteoarthritis, are due to the excess wear and tear the extra weight puts on the spine, hips and knees. Others, like gall stones and diabetes, coronary artery disease and stroke, are due to the changes obesity produces in the body chemistry. Life-threatening illnesses are not only more common, but more often fatal, among those who are overweight. Cancer, particularly some of the commonest types – breast, colon and prostate – is associated with being overweight.

Weight and health

Clearly, being the right weight is a very important part of being healthy, as well as of looking good. If you put health first and weight second, you will find that the weight eventually normalises, but it just doesn't seem to work the other way round. In the long run, adequate exercise and a positive cheerful outlook are as important as diet for good health and lasting weight control. Achieving the right weight should be part of an ongoing life plan and not just an isolated scheme for a few weeks. 'I must lose weight for the holidays' is not the motivation for lasting success!

If you want to maximise your health, it is absolutely essential to be in control of what you eat. You cannot allow the taste, sight or remembrance of a food to dictate what you eat. Many weight-control programmes fail because they don't retrain your thinking about food. Clearly, if you make an enormous effort of self-discipline and deny yourself cream cakes and chocolate, you may lose weight – but continue to think longingly of them, and you are unlikely to resist the urge to eat them when you have got your weight down. Sadly, if that's the case, as so many can testify, your weight won't stay down.

Being the right weight involves the whole person, not just the eating habits. Spiritual factors are important too, especially coming to terms with oneself and one's place in creation. Even in the twenty-first century, the Bible has many valuable insights about health, food and weight. It tells the story of a loving God who prepared a perfect and beautiful world for His children. Everything was made according to His plan. He designed their bodies and planned their work and recreation, environment, food and companionship, which He Himself would share. The closer we can get to the original principles, including the original plant food diet and physically active life, *and* the communion with the Creator, the better our health will be, and that applies to our weight as well.

What is your right weight?

The first thing in weight control is to come to terms with one's body type, and then to concentrate on getting healthy – because optimum health will ultimately lead to the right weight. This applies to both underweight and overweight people.

The human body is a masterpiece of design, the crowning work of God's creation – and, like any machine, it works best when the maker's instructions are followed. Many people are unhappy with their bodies, not appreciating the wonder of the overall design and the variations that are normal. Some are designed to be below average weight, some above, but definitely none are intended to be obese – 20% or more above the recommended healthy weight. Some people put on weight much more easily than others. Their metabolism is very economical, and they burn less energy and have extra left over to store. Others have a different metabolism that tends to burn at a higher rate, and they just never seem to get fat, no matter what they eat. Actual endocrine disturbances, for example thyroid deficiency, that cause weight gain are rather rare. For most people with a weight problem, the solution is not *medication* so much as *dedication*! Following the rules of health (the divine plan) will enable each person to reach his or her full physical potential.

Exercise

One of the most important parts of any health plan is exercise. Weight is not a problem for the Masai tribesmen in East Africa, who spend all day on the run with their cattle, or with the Hunza in Northern Pakistan, who walk up and down mountains all day. We are designed to be active, not to be sitting all day, and we are at our best when we get vigorous activity. One reason why some people don't lose weight, even on the most frugal diets, is that exercise is necessary to stimulate the body to burn up the calories and to activate the appetite control centre in the brain. *Regular* exercise is vital for weight control: not sport once a week or a walk on Sundays, but regular *daily* exercise. Few exercises can beat walking for safety and convenience. Several miles a day would be good, with a gradual increase in speed and duration. No time for exercise? Take the long-term view. The investment of time for daily exercise from now on may add several extra years of healthy life. And incidentally, it's the exercise you enjoy that does you the most good – so find something you really like doing.

Diet and weight

For good health and weight control you need to eat the **right amount** of the **right kind** of food at the **right time** in the **right frame of mind**.

The amount of food needed to satisfy the appetite depends very much on the kind of food. The more natural the food, the more fibre it will contain, and the more fibre, the more filling it is. The fibre makes it bulky, and the bulk fills the stomach and makes us feel satisfied. Also, the more fibre, the more chewy it usually is, and quite a lot of the satisfaction depends on the amount of time the food spends in the mouth. Soft, smooth foods like ice cream or chocolate mousse go down very quickly, and aren't very satisfying. It's the same with white bread. Its chewy fibre has been removed, and it doesn't satisfy the way wholewheat bread does. Eating very quickly also leads to overeating; whereas eating slowly, savouring each mouthful and chewing it well, increases the level of satisfaction. White bread, as well as being less filling, has more calories – two good reasons to choose wholewheat bread. Here is another example: about ten raw apples have the same number of calories as one piece of apple pie with ice cream. Raw apples are much more filling: who would want to chew their way through more than five? But a person could well have a double helping of pie and ice cream!

You stay the same weight when the energy in the food you eat equals the energy you use up. Clearly, if the energy output is low and the food intake is high, there's going to be a surplus to be stored away as fat. This is the case with the typical high-fat Western diet, in which 40-45% of the calories come from fat, and as much as 80-90% of the food may be refined. Most slimming diets try to solve the problem by reducing the food intake to below the supposed energy output so that the stored fat is mobilised and used up. Unfortunately, these low-calorie diets are unsatisfying and demand more willpower than most people have. If the food intake is really low, the body goes into **starvation mode**, where metabolism slows down and the body conserves every possible calorie – breaking down muscle tissue as well as fat, endangering health, and making weight loss very difficult.

What **kind** of food? **Whole plant foods** win hands-down every time. They are more bulky, so you feel fuller and more satisfied. They have their full complement of vitamins and minerals, and they don't contain excess calories. Refined foods have less bulk, are less filling and have more calories. Excess calorie intake is almost inevitable when these foods form a large part of the diet. In addition, they are deficient in the vitamins, minerals and phytochemicals that the body needs to metabolise all those calories and to fight disease. The absence of these things creates even more dissatisfaction, and can produce cravings and addictions as well.

Fat provides more than twice as many calories per gram as carbohydrates and protein, so it makes sense to eat less of it, but in itself fat is not bad. In the right amount, as found in natural, unrefined plant foods, it is good. Some is necessary to enable us to absorb the fat-soluble vitamins, and it adds flavour and interest to the diet. A varied diet of unrefined plant foods is not a fat-free diet, and need not even be a very low-fat diet. There are plenty of healthy natural fats in nuts, seeds, olives and avocados. It's not these (in moderate amounts) that cause the problems: it's the *added* fats. A very overweight person would be wise to be careful not to use too much of even natural high-fat foods, but few should cut them out completely without expert advice.

The paradox of low-fat foods

The food industry has had great success with the sale of low-fat food, but it has actually been found that people get fatter when they use these foods. This is because fat gives a feeling of satisfaction, limiting the intake; what happens is that we eat larger amounts of the low-fat foods; the *total* number of calories is higher, so the weight goes up. Low-fat sweet things are *extra* high in sugar. Low-fat spreads may not be much help either, especially if you eat them in double the quantity of the old full-fat spreads.

Two dangerous dietary myths need to be exploded

One is that high-protein diets are the way to lose weight. While it is true that the metabolism of protein uses extra energy and that high-protein diets can result in rapid weight loss, it's at a price. High protein intake puts stress on the liver, kidneys and heart. The other myth is that starchy foods like bread and potatoes are fattening. Unrefined starchy foods are filling and prevent overeating, so the opposite is true: though of course bread becomes fattening when thickly spread with butter and jam, as do potatoes when they are made into chips.

What about animal products?

Even apart from the question of the association of animal foods with degenerative disease, they are not the best for a health-promoting diet, especially a weight-reducing one. They tend to be concentrated foods, high in calories, fat and protein. They contain no fibre, and often contain large amounts of fat. If they are used, it should be in small amounts, and preferably the low-fat varieties. A varied whole plant food diet based on unrefined starches – with plenty of fruit and vegetables, and also some pulses, nuts and seeds – is the most effective for weight loss.

What about drinks?

They can be the worst enemies in the battle for weight control. Fizzy soft drinks are mainly sugared water. Alcoholic drinks are even worse, because alcohol itself is a rich source of empty calories. Even natural fruit juices are high in calories. The best drink for weight control is definitely water. Tea and coffee don't contain calories, unless sugar, milk or cream are added, but caffeine is a drug with withdrawal effects, a feeling of let-down that can be confused with hunger, and makes appetite control more difficult.

Should we count calories?

Absolutely not! If we choose a varied, unrefined, mainly plant food diet, there is no need for this tedious exercise. The principle is to eat enough healthy food to feel satisfied, and to exercise enough to raise the metabolism enough to burn it up.

The time to eat

A regular programme is one of the secrets of appetite and weight control. A large, filling breakfast will set you up for the day and eliminate the need for between-meal snacks (which are usually high-fat or high-sugar). Make a decision not to eat between meals, and save yourself the trouble of having to make a decision every time you are tempted.

Food eaten in the morning tends to be burned up during the course of the day's activities. Two groups of young male volunteers were given one identical meal a day for two weeks, the one difference being that group A ate their meal for breakfast and group B ate their meal for supper. Group A lost weight; group B gained. The groups were then reversed, with the same result. Why? Because food eaten at night tends to be stored as fat; food eaten in the morning gets used up. Moral: eat a big breakfast, a moderate lunch and a small evening meal. The old adage 'breakfast like a king, lunch like a prince, sup like a pauper' is especially valid for those who are battling with their weight. Those who are seriously overweight would be wise to miss the evening meal altogether.

The frame of mind in which we eat

This is important too. It's very easy to eat for emotional reasons. Lonely and sad people who feel rejected often eat for comfort; and, unfortunately, comfort foods are usually high in sugar and fat. Self-respect and self-acceptance are healthy emotions at mealtimes, along with acceptance of the laws of life and a thankful heart. It's vital to cultivate interests in subjects other than food, and to take an active interest in other people and their problems as well as our own.

Improving one's health and correcting one's weight both need to be long-term projects.

Usually it has taken years to gain the excess weight, and the best way is to reduce it slowly, sometimes over several years. Most diets aim at a loss of two pounds per week, but a steady, half-pound-a-week loss will add up to nearly two stones a year. The diet and lifestyle changes that are made gradually will be more easy to maintain, unlike the usual slimming diet with its promised quick results but short-lived success. The healthy *lifestyle* needs to be *lifelong*.

What motivation is needed for a lasting change of lifestyle and eating habits?

Gratitude to the God who created the human race in His image, designing our bodies for maximum enjoyment of life, our food for maximum health and enjoyment of eating, and our spirit for communion with Him, is the best motivation one can have.

Practical suggestions for starting a weight-reduction programme

Those who are very overweight and are unwell, very easily tired or short of breath, or are on regular medication, should of course consult their medical advisors in case there are any specific restrictions for them. They should also take advice before starting exercise programmes or fasting. For them it's even more important to start exercise changes gradually, but some will find it helpful to start their new eating programme with a therapeutic diet, even beginning with a one- or two-day fast.

If you start with a **fast**, keep to a normal daily programme with fruit or vegetable juices or herbal teas at your normal mealtimes. Drink plenty of extra water between mealtimes. Do light exercise only, and have as interesting a programme as possible to keep your mind off food. Many people who have tried it say that fasting is actually easier than eating less. Abstaining from food and drinking lots of fluids have a cleansing effect that produces a feeling of well-being, a relish for healthy food once the fast is over, and a distinct confidence in your ability to control your appetite!

A regular daily programme

The best way to start the day is to get up early and to have a large drink of water or herbal tea, at least half an hour before breakfast. This stimulates the kidneys to get rid of the night's waste products, and gets the metabolism off to a good start. You could open the window and breathe some fresh air or do a few exercises while the kettle boils. Have a good, filling breakfast. It's the most important meal of the day, and you should enjoy it! Sometime during the day fit in some extra exercise, and do it as briskly as you can. Walking is always a safe exercise for everyone who is actually able to walk. Have your other main meal at midday if possible, and have a small, light evening meal several hours before bedtime.

Either at the start of your diet plan, or after your short one- or two-day fast, you could have a **fruit diet** for three days. Eat all the fruit you want – of any kind, provided you don't add sugar – and drink lots of water between meals. Fruit juices contain quite a lot of nutrition and are best at mealtimes.

Follow this with a three-day **fruit and vegetable** regime. Start with a selection of fruit for breakfast; have a selection of vegetables for lunch, starting with a salad, and including filling things like jacket potatoes if you want to – but don't add any butter or other high-fat dressings. For supper have another fruit meal.

After two or three days on the fruit and vegetable regime, you can start to add some wholewheat bread or other cereal food to the fruit meals. Choose a kind of bread that is tasty enough to be eaten without the usual high-fat spreads.

The next stage is to get onto a **normal whole plant food diet**, and it's worth keeping this up for a month – or, better still, indefinitely. Add some high-protein plant foods to each meal: beans or lentils, or dishes or spreads containing nuts and seeds. It's best to avoid all the refined foods. This includes many of the ready-prepared vegetarian foods, too. What about olive oil? Most people can allow small amounts if it makes it easier to eat salad.

Regular whole-food diet suggestions

Variety
This is an important key to good health, because it ensures an adequate supply of all the essential nutrients, which in turn protects against food cravings and other problems.

In general it's a good plan to eat fruits and vegetables at separate meals. Some find them much easier to digest this way; others find that it's easier not to overeat if there is less variety at any one meal. On the other hand, it is important to have a wide variety of food from day to day.

Breakfast
Many people find it's nice to start the day with a 'fruit and grain' meal – like fresh fruit, cereal and toast. Start with a couple of pieces of fruit. Choose cereals made from whole wheat or other grains without added sugar. You don't have to eat them with milk; you can use fresh or cooked fruit, nut or soya milk (which tastes a lot more creamy than skimmed milk). Raw grains are hard to digest, except oats, which are quite digestible if soaked overnight. Hot breakfast cereals can be made from a variety of flaked whole grains. Sweeten them with raisins or chopped dates rather than sugar.

Develop a taste for spreads that contain their full spectrum of nutrition – whole-nut butters, tahini, avocado (which is an excellent substitute for cream cheese), mashed banana. Delicious 'jams' can be very easily made from dried fruits, cooked and mashed or blended. Then you won't need butter with its cholesterol and saturated fat, or margarine, which is just as high in fat as butter, or even 'low-fat' spreads, which are still 50% fat at least. Savoury breakfasts are good too, as long as they keep to the principle of avoiding refined and deficient foods.

Lunch
This should *ideally* be the other main meal. Start with a big salad: and the more weight to be lost, the bigger and chewier the salad should be. Base the meal on unrefined starch: potato, brown rice or pasta, maize or whatever. Add cooked vegetables and a smaller helping of the high-protein food. Chicken and fish are preferable to red meat, but vegetarian foods, especially the beans and lentils, are best. Beware of adding fat or high-fat sauces.

The evening meal
It is best to have the smallest meal in the evening if it's possible. Bread and spread is a good evening menu, with a vegetable soup or salad or with fruit. Or what about an evening fast? Omitting the evening meal for a few days or weeks can help to get a serious start to dealing with a serious weight problem.

What if you can't choose the menu?

If you don't have any say about what happens in the kitchen you can still make choices that will improve your diet and health.

First, don't add sugar and avoid all sugar-rich foods. Get your own supplies of other foods, such as fruits or nuts, to take their place if possible.

Be very careful about fats. Cultivate a taste for less. Remember, fats come on bread as butter and margarine, and are plentiful in fried food – but are also present in large amounts in many gravies, sauces and made-up dishes such as stews and casseroles. Pastry is by weight at least one-third fat, and cakes, biscuits and ice creams are often as rich in fats as they are in sugar. Be careful about cheese – standard hard cheeses like cheddar are over fifty percent fat.

Eat bigger helpings of the vegetables and salads, and smaller helpings of the high-fat foods, avoiding the richest altogether. This will save you many empty calories.

And do work hard on the exercise programme too.

How strict do I have to be?

This is something you need to decide for yourself, according to how much weight you need to lose, how well your regime is going, how good your general health is, what your social circumstances are and so on. Occasional deviations from your healthy eating plan may be unavoidable, and should not cause any pangs of guilt: but frequent indulgence in junk food makes it more difficult to develop a taste for the good things. As time passes, if you manage to avoid the dangerous fattening foods, you will find that you develop a taste for the healthy food. As you start to feel better on the new regime, you are even more motivated to continue it. Some people find that it is best to be total abstainers from rich cakes and puddings, because if they start, it may set off a craving that is difficult to control. Others can take them or leave them and are able to enjoy the occasional junk-food meal on social occasions. The problem is when one feels the need to eat junk food to reward oneself for abstaining from it! That is likely to lead to the slippery slope of failure.

9 Staying fit and flexible

'Well,' you may say, 'fit for what?'

Clearly what is fit for Father may not be fit for Grandfather – or Grandmother, for that matter. But there is an approach to maintaining fitness without the element of risk.

Primarily we should define personal fitness in the following terms: that we are able to carry out the tasks that have to be done; that we are able to become involved in activities that, within reason, we like to do – in the first instance without stress or strain, and in the second in an acceptable and controllable amount.

The human body is basically a machine, which, by definition, means that it is 'a device for doing work'.

The simplest of all machines are levers and we use them constantly. For example, the garden spade is a simple lever with a weight to be moved at one end (the soil), a fulcrum in the middle (one hand gripping the lever) and the other hand exerting downward force on the spade handle. If the 'lifting hand' (fulcrum) slides up the shaft away from the weight to be lifted towards the handle, the soil appears to become heavier and heavier, so requiring more and more effort to raise it.

The human body is a system of levers. For instance, the long bones in the arm and the forearm, thigh and leg are rigid lines and each moves at a joint, which is the fulcrum. Weight is moved on these bones – the body weight in particular on the lower limbs – on the upper limbs a large variety of weighty objects from saucepans to suitcases, from furniture to younger members of the family, and the effort (force) needed to move these weights is produced by the contraction of muscles.

For the most part the arrangement is such that the muscles are attached and therefore apply a force between the weight on the limbs and the joints, and furthermore much closer to the joints than to the weight. This compares with using a garden spade with hands close together – consequently a great deal of effort is needed and one will be aware of the stress involved. Nevertheless, it is an impressive thought that the human machine functions on average for a little more than threescore years and ten, whereas those devices that we normally think of as machines rarely match this longevity.

Machines must be maintained; they must be cared for – they must be serviced. Clearly there is a need for freely-moving joints; for muscles which produce sufficient force to move the weights that they act upon; and furthermore there is a need for an adequate supply of energy. Unlike muscle tissue, joint surfaces have a very limited blood supply and, for the most part, gain nourishment – energy – by absorbing fluid. This simply means that cartilage takes up fluid in the same way that a bath sponge takes up water when squeezed and released. When movement occurs, some parts of the cartilagenous joint surface are compressed and other parts decompressed. Movement in the opposite direction reverses this effect and so consequently it is during the movement of a joint that the cartilage gains its nutritive requirements. Further to this need, surrounding the joints are capsular ligaments and unless they are regularly stretched they will shrink, thus reducing the range of movement possible and so in turn leading to a reduction of cartilagenous nutrition. Unless a full range of movements is regularly carried out, normal complete movements will become less. Enquire of the older members of the family as to whether or not they can stretch their arms in a straight line above the head – or perhaps produce a straight back!

Muscles, on the other hand, receive their nutritive supply through the blood capillaries within them; and in this context it is useful to consider the question of an effective circulation. Circulation is dependent on three resources:

- the heart itself;
- the respiratory pump; and
- skeletal muscular activity.

Although the heart does pump blood around the body, by itself it is not maximally efficient. Separating the thorax from the abdomen is a thin sheet of muscle in the shape of a dome, which is called the diaphragm. When it contracts the dome descends, the thorax (chest) is enlarged and the abdomen is compressed. As a result of this, the air pressure in the lungs is reduced, and as atmospheric pressure is greater, air moves into the lungs – and so we breathe in. But at the same time the pressure on the blood in the abdomen is increased and consequently this causes the blood to flow into the thorax via the large vein to the heart. Therefore, it will be seen that effective breathing is not only essential for good ventilation of the lungs, but it is also essential for circulating the blood back to the heart. Within the muscles of the body are soft-walled veins, and when muscles contract, these veins are compressed and the blood within squeezed out and moved towards the heart.

Consequently, effective breathing and muscular activity increases the venous return to the heart. When the pressure in the large veins is increased, a reflex mechanism is activated which causes the rate and force of the heart activity to increase and so pump the blood onwards via the arteries to the lungs and the body as a whole. Muscular strength is dependent upon the work that muscles are required to do, and as the heart is a muscle, general muscular activity will give the heart more work to do. Under controlled circumstances exercises can improve the mechanism of the body as a whole. It becomes clear that in order to maintain this mechanism, the following are needed:

- freely-moving joints;
- sufficient muscular strength to move the levers; and
- an effective circulation in order to supply the energy needed.

Whereas this requirement applies to all structures, certain joints and muscles are particularly vulnerable to wear. As the years go by, joints which tend to be affected are the shoulder, hip, and spine, and this is because in our everyday activities we do not move them through the full range of normal movement. It is therefore useful to do the following exercises at regular intervals.

The human body is basically a machine, which, by definition, means that it is 'a device for doing work'.

Mobility exercises

So the first requirement for physical fitness is to maintain full range of movement in the joints of the body. In the achievement of this there will, of course, be muscular activity and therefore a certain degree of muscular strength will also be maintained.

1 Neck and shoulders
Stand relaxed and hold the wrist behind the back. Gently pull the shoulder down and across and tip the head away.

2 Neck and upper back
Kneel on all fours with your back straight. Keep your abdominal muscles tight. Lift up through your spine to round your back, then gently release.

3 Shoulders and chest

Stand up straight and place your hands behind your head. Gently pull your elbows back and push your chest forward.

4 Shoulders and chest

Start with your hands by your sides. Slowly raise to shoulder height and then gently lower back to starting point.

5 Spinal stretch

Kneel on all fours. Align your hips over your knees. Slide your hands forwards but do not allow your hips to move. Allow your chest to drop towards the floor.

7 Hip rotation

Bear your weight on one leg. Align knee of other leg with the midline of foot and rotate gently from the hip.

8 Hip strength

Lie on your side, supporting head on hand. Bend body slightly at the hip. Keep body weight forward. Raise and lower the leg.

6 Spinal stretch

Lie down, face up with knees bent and feet flat on the floor. One at a time, gently bring your knees to your chest and hold.

Starting your exercise programme

Do I need to exercise? Yes. Whatever your lifestyle, current physical health, age or gender, you can benefit from regular exercise. You are never too young, too old, or too unfit to get started.

Set yourself a goal. If you're serious about improving your overall physical health, you should be working towards doing at least thirty minutes of exercise at least three times a week. (Better still if you can manage the same amount of exercise every day of the week.)

Take it steady. If you're planning to turn over a new leaf and start an exercise programme where previously your lifestyle was largely inactive, recognise that you should start as you mean to go on – at your own pace. (If your own pace requires you to stop for a cake every ten minutes you should review your strategy!)

Your heart needs a workout too

It is a good idea to get involved in some sort of general exercise or sport which provides both cardiovascular and muscular workout – for example, brisk walking, swimming, cycling, tennis, badminton, basketball and similar pursuits. Consequently, each individual should make an appropriate selection in terms of age, interest and availability.

General advice

Nevertheless, in starting any activity the same ground rules should be followed, and these are:
- start with the minimum effort; and
- progress in a gradual manner.

For example, take walking. In accordance with your present ability, you could start with a hundred yards, the following day walk twice the distance, and so on, and in case it is thought that this goes on ad infinitum, an average daily stint of about half an hour should be considered reasonable.

Never overstress or overfatigue the body. Sufficient work should be done to experience an increase in heart and respiratory rate, but this rate should return to normal within a few minutes after the effort ceases. But there again it is not recommended that the pulse should be checked at frequent intervals, and anyway it is difficult to check the respiratory rate for oneself.

It is essential to enjoy what you have decided to do. It should not be done just because 'it is good for you'.

Graduated, regular physical activity will build up muscle strength, improve circulatory efficiency and consequently increase our ability to withstand and tolerate the normal everyday stresses that we all have to put up with.

Warm-ups and cool-downs

It is good to recognise the importance of warming up before commencing a period of physical exertion. Likewise it is good exercise practice to decrease the effort required towards the end of your workout as a cooling-down period.

'The idea behind warming up is to prepare the muscles for physical activity,' says Ben Kibbler, MD, director of the Lexington Clinic Sports Medicine Center, Kentucky. 'You want to improve flexibility, strength, extensibility of the tendons and blood flow to the muscles. A muscle in a resting state has a certain length. Warming up improves the ability to move the muscle through its entire range of motion without injury. While warmth applied to the outside of the body warms the skin and parts of the muscles close to the skin's surface, it doesn't effectively warm the muscles, particularly the deep-seated muscles and tendons.' – *fitnessonline.com*.

Safe stretches

The following stretches can be done as part of a 'warm-up' regime or after activity as a 'cool-down'. Stretching can also be used as a workout in its own right for thirty minutes, three times a week. For maximum benefit stretches should be held for twenty to thirty seconds at the point of comfortable tension. Always be sure to stretch both sides of the body. Remember too, it is advisable to consult a physician prior to starting any exercise programme. Always drink water before, during and after exercise to remain hydrated.

Breathing

This breathing exercise can be done either standing or lying down. Inhale and fill the lungs; allow the chest and stomach to expand. Exhale and allow the chest and stomach to fall. Concentrate on pulling your navel towards your spine while exhaling.

Posture and neutral spine

Before beginning any exercise programme it is important to find the most stable position for your spine.

Rock your pelvis forwards, then back, and then find the mid-point, which should encourage a natural curve in your lower back. Hold this position. This is the neutral position for your spine, the central position for good posture.

Triceps stretch

3 Lift the elbow above the head and drop the forearm behind the head. Slide the forearm down the middle of the back. Support the elbow with the opposite hand and apply gentle pressure.

Back and shoulders

4 Stand with knees slightly bent. Leaning forwards, grasp the back of the thighs. Pull away from the legs, leading with the upper back. Keep the head in a neutral position.

Trunk stretch

5 Lie on your front with elbows tucked into the side of your body. Gently lift the upper body, pressing the chest up and forwards. Keep your elbows on the floor.

Spine stretch

6 Lie on your back with your spine in the neutral position. Gently bring one knee towards the chest and hold. Bring your other knee to the chest and hold.

Groin stretch

7 Support your body on all fours and slowly extend one leg to the side. Press the groin towards the floor while leaning back slightly.

Calf stretch

8 Stand relaxed and step one foot behind as far as comfort will allow. Lean forwards, keeping ankle and knee of the back leg in a straight line with the hips and shoulder. Check the front knee is over the shoelaces. Rest hands on knee.

107

Hip flexor stretch

Kneel down, take one foot forwards as far as comfort allows. Gently lean forwards, pressing the groin forwards and towards the floor. Align the front knee directly over the ankle or shoelace.

Lying quadricep stretch

Lying on your side, support the body by resting the head on the hand or upper arm. Angle the bottom leg forwards and bend slightly to aid balance. Bend the top leg and take the foot behind, holding the ankle with your hand. Press hips forwards. Keep knees parallel with floor.

Abdominal muscles

Start by lying face-down with your spine in the neutral position. Lift the hips off the floor, keep your abdominal muscles firm and hold the position for as long as is possible. Do not allow the lower back to sag. To increase intensity, lift the knees off the floor.

Abdominal muscles

Lying down face-up, bend the knees and gradually curl the upper body no more than 30-40 degrees. Keep the lower back on the floor. Focus on contracting the abdominal muscles.

What exercise can do for you*

It increases the efficiency of your lungs, conditioning them to process more air with less effort.

It increases the efficiency of your heart in several ways. It grows stronger and pumps more blood with each stroke, reducing the number of strokes necessary.

It increases the number and size of your blood vessels as well as your total blood volume, thus saturating the tissue throughout the body with energy-producing oxygen.

It increases your body's maximal oxygen consumption by increasing the efficiency of the means of supply and delivery. In doing so, it improves the overall condition of your body, especially its most important parts – the lungs, the heart, the blood vessels and the body tissue – giving you protection against many forms of illness and disease.

It improves the tone of your muscles and blood vessels, changing them from weak and flabby tissue to strong and firm tissue, often reducing blood pressure in the process.

It slows down your ageing process and physical deterioration as it restores your zest for life and youthful activity.

It may change your whole outlook on life. You learn to relax, develop a better self-image, and tolerate the stress of daily living. You will sleep better and get more work done with less fatigue.

*From *The New Aerobics* by Kenneth Cooper, MD, Bantam Books

10 Good news about cancer

The first piece of good news about cancer is that a great deal is known about what causes it, which means that a great deal is known about how to prevent it. For example, the World Cancer Research Fund (WCRF) indicates that about a third of common cancers could be prevented by eating a healthy diet, maintaining a healthy weight and taking regular physical exercise. (See the WCRF/AICR's Second Expert Report, *Food, Nutrition, Physical Activity, and the Prevention of Cancer: A Global Perspective* [2007].) The second piece of good news is that, for many cancers, treatments are now much more successful – which means that many people with cancer are surviving for much longer than was possible a few decades ago.

Worldwide cancer incidence doubled between 1975 and 2000. Since 2000, the incidence of cancer decreased a little in some areas, probably mainly due to people smoking less. Unfortunately, the World Cancer Report 2014 published by the WHO indicates that worldwide cancer cases are on the increase, and that we should expect a 70% increase by 2034. From what we now know, the steady rise in cancer incidence of the past decades could be completely reversed if enough people were willing to make the necessary simple lifestyle changes.

It was back in the 1950s that Richard Doll and Austen Bradford Hill drew the world's attention to the connection between smoking and lung cancer. At that time little was known about the causes of cancer and there were few effective treatments. Worse still, in many places a conspiracy of silence surrounded the whole topic: some people did recover, often after extensive surgery, but usually it was the fatal cases one heard about. People dreaded cancer even more then than they do now.

Scientists now discover new facts about the causes of cancer almost every day. Most of these relate to avoidable factors, which means that individuals can make choices that will help them to avoid it. Few causes of cancer are as clear-cut as smoking, and it has taken many years to disentangle them. The task is by no means over, but there is now overwhelming evidence that other lifestyle factors, such as diet, lack of exercise, alcohol and drugs, are important in producing cancer too. As most of these factors are avoidable, it means that a great many cancers are potentially avoidable too.

Several decades ago epidemiologists started mapping the incidence of cancer. They found great variations between countries, within countries, and even from one town to another. This confirmed the importance of these environmental and lifestyle factors, and that, because many could be avoided, prevention was possible. Dr T. Colin Campbell studied liver cancer, known to be caused by a toxin in mouldy peanuts. This was a common problem in children in the hot and humid Philippines, where it was difficult to store foods. He had expected to find that the 'undernourished' children with low-protein diets would be the most likely to develop cancer. He was surprised to discover, however, that the children on the highest-protein diets were the ones who developed it, while those on low-protein plant food diets did not develop it. Following up this finding with animal studies, he found that the cancer could be 'switched' on or off by altering the amount of animal protein in the diet. These and subsequent studies, by Dr Campbell and many others, have shown that a whole, unrefined, unprocessed plant food diet poses the lowest risk of cancer.

Cancer is commonest in the rich developed countries, particularly in Western Europe, North America and Australia. These are countries with a high proportion of animal products in their diets. Here, cancers of the breast, lung, colon and prostate are particularly common. North America and Europe, with less than 20% of the world's population, have nearly 50% of the world's cancer.

Africa is still the area with the lowest cancer incidence, with 14% of the world's population and only 4% of the cancer. However, Africa is catching up – and an international conference in 2007 warned that, as more Africans start smoking and adopt the overfed sedentary Western lifestyle, they are developing more of the rich countries' cancers, in addition to their own burden of cancers due to infective agents, including HIV/AIDS. This is serious, because in many parts of Africa medical services are already severely stretched.

What is cancer?

Cancer is not a single disease – there are at least 200 different types. It starts when cells start to multiply uncontrollably, forming a mass or tumour, which eventually invades surrounding tissues and can spread via blood or lymph circulation to more distant parts of the body. (Benign tumours do not invade other tissues, but where there is no medical care benign tumours can cause serious problems by their size and the pressure they put on surrounding organs.)

How does cancer start?

Probably our bodies produce cancer cells all the time, especially as we get older, but our immune systems destroy them before they cause trouble. In each person there is a balance between the causes of disease and the body's defences. When the defences are in control, cancer cells are destroyed. When they fail, cancer cells start to multiply. It may take many years before the defences fail, and many years after that before the cancer is even big enough to be felt. It is estimated that cancers double in size every 100 days; starting with a single cancer cell, it could take years to reach the size of a pea, but only another year or so to reach the size of an egg.

What are the body's defences?

The body has a very complex and efficient system for defending itself against infections and dangerous materials, whether they come from inside or outside the body. The skin and mucous membranes that line the body's entrances and exits are the first line of defence against bacteria and other invaders. The second line is the cells of the immune system, the army of white blood cells. These cells are the front-line defenders against internal threats like cancer cells. Some swallow up the enemies; others produce chemicals to kill them.

The immune system is very important in the fight against cancer, but cancer itself can weaken it, and so can some cancer treatments.

How to strengthen the body's defences?

Regular active exercise, regular and adequate sleep and rest, regular moderate sunshine, the avoidance of poisons, and, of course, a healthy diet all strengthen the immune system. The most effective diet is based on a variety of whole, unrefined plant foods with their antioxidant anti-cancer properties intact.

What weakens the body's defences? Here are the things to avoid:

Smoking
It lowers resistance to disease in general, and the carcinogens in tobacco tar actively promote cancer. Cannabis smoking has similar dangers.

Alcohol
It lowers the resistance to most forms of ill health, particularly cancer. Cancer of the oesophagus, mouth and throat are all associated with heavy drinking, but even as few as one or two drinks a day increases the risk of breast cancer.

Obesity
Obesity is a contributing factor to the most common reproductive system cancers, to colon cancer and to others too.

Lack of exercise
This is because exercise stimulates the immune system.

A high-fat, high-sugar, refined food diet
The large amounts of empty calories burden and deprive the body, as well as encouraging obesity.

Animal produce, especially red meat and preserved and processed meats
This includes bacon and sausages, which are associated with higher incidence of bowel and other cancers.

Irregular hours; lack of sleep
This is because the defence system is maintained and repaired while we sleep, and the process is most efficient at night and in the dark. Shift workers have many extra health problems, including more cancer.

Stress and other negative emotions
They all depress the immune system.

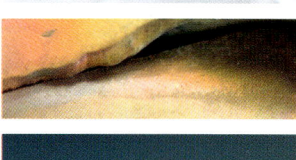

Carcinogens (cancer-producing chemicals)
The dangers associated with such carcinogens as asbestos and dry-cleaning fluids, tobacco tar and mouldy peanut toxin are well-known. Some food additives, such as preservatives and flavour enhancers, pesticides, and other chemicals used in the production and marketing of food, are a concern, too. However, the current consensus opinion of the main cancer organisations and the World Health Organisation is that apart from those who are heavily exposed to them at work, only 1-2% of cancers can be reliably linked to these substances.

About 6% of cancers are reliably linked to industrial causes, mainly in the developing countries where industrial processes are less well controlled.

Hormone imbalances help to trigger the reproductive cancers, and obesity raises oestrogen and other reproductive hormone levels.

What sets the process of cancer off?

There are many factors involved in every case of this complex disease. Something – such as a virus, a carcinogenic chemical or radiation exposure – changes the DNA in a cell nucleus, causing it to divide excessively. If the immune system is in good form, it will quickly destroy the rogue cells, but if the harm is repeated many times, and if the immune system is weak, the cancer cells eventually win.

Who gets cancer?

On the one side are the pro-cancer factors – carcinogens in the environment or the diet, excessive exposure to sun, an inherited tendency to cancer – and even one's temperament and attitude are important. On the other side are the anti-cancer factors – a healthy environment and lifestyle, a good inherited constitution and an optimistic attitude.

Lung cancer is an example. Fewer than one in ten smokers will get lung cancer, and smokers who exercise and eat healthily are at lower risk.

The majority of cancer sufferers are over 65 – it's mainly a disease of old age. Currently, one in three people in the rich countries of the West will develop cancer, and one in four will die of it. With early diagnosis and prompt treatment, many people will recover completely. For others, with the right treatment, their cancer will be a chronic disease with which they will be able to live for many years.

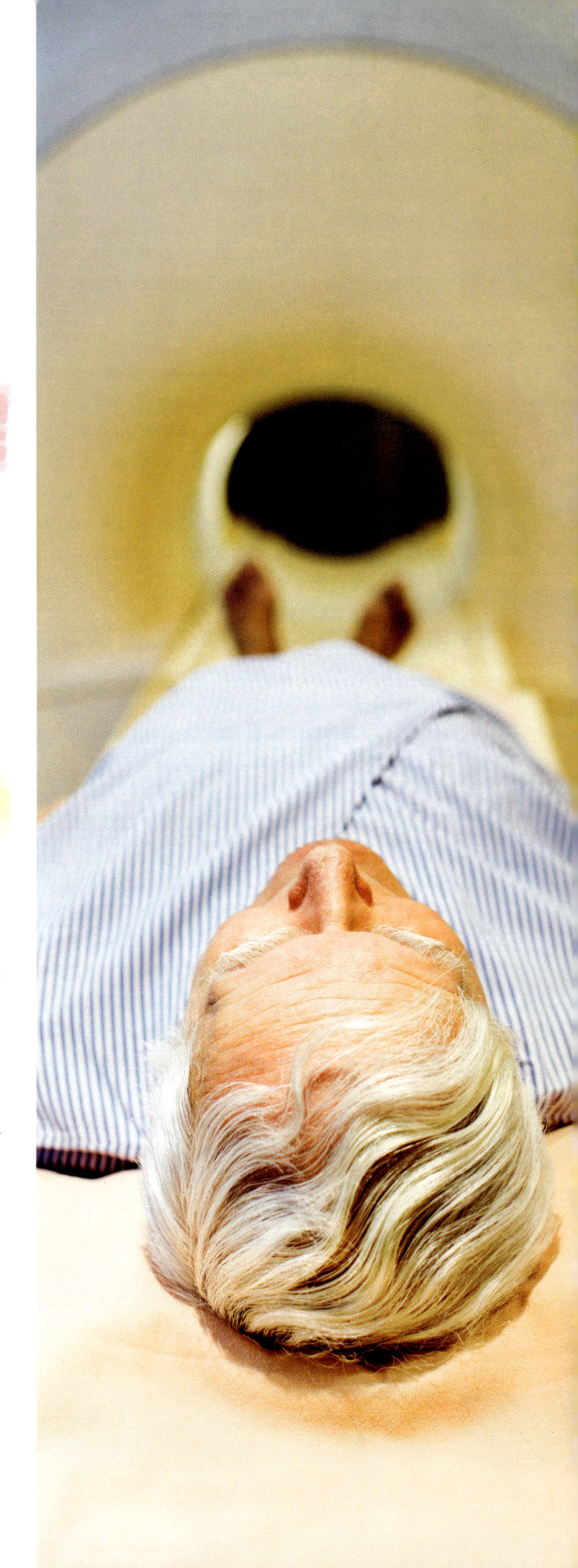

Infections and cancer

Fifty years ago the idea that germs caused cancer was ridiculed, but we now know that many cancers are associated with viruses and other micro-organisms. However, infection is unlikely ever to be the result of only one factor – lifestyle, environment and heredity play their part as well.

Genes and cancer

The current view is that several hundred of our estimated 20,000-25,000 genes are involved with cancer. Oncogenes are genes which should control cell division, but have gone wrong and promote cancer formation. Tumour-suppressor genes slow down cell division and repair the damaged DNA of the oncogenes.

What makes the genes go wrong? The simple answer: lifestyle, environment and heredity factors. This is actually good news, because we have many choices that we can make about the first two. Fewer than 10% of cancers are thought to be hereditary, and even in these cases lifestyle makes a difference.

Dean Ornish studied a group of men who had decided against medical treatment for their early low-risk prostate cancer. They agreed to be randomly selected to either continue their normal regime or follow a comprehensive lifestyle programme that included a low-fat unrefined plant food diet, regular exercise and relaxation therapy. Cancer biopsies were taken from both groups at the start and after three months. Genetic studies of the biopsies showed that several hundred genes were involved in the cancers, and that, in those in the lifestyle programme group, oncogenes were 'turned off' and cancer-suppressor genes were 'turned on'. This is very interesting evidence that lifestyle actually affects genes and offers more hope for cancer sufferers. An estimated 5-10% of cancers are hereditary, and this research suggests that even hereditary cancers can be postponed or even avoided altogether by lifestyle choices.

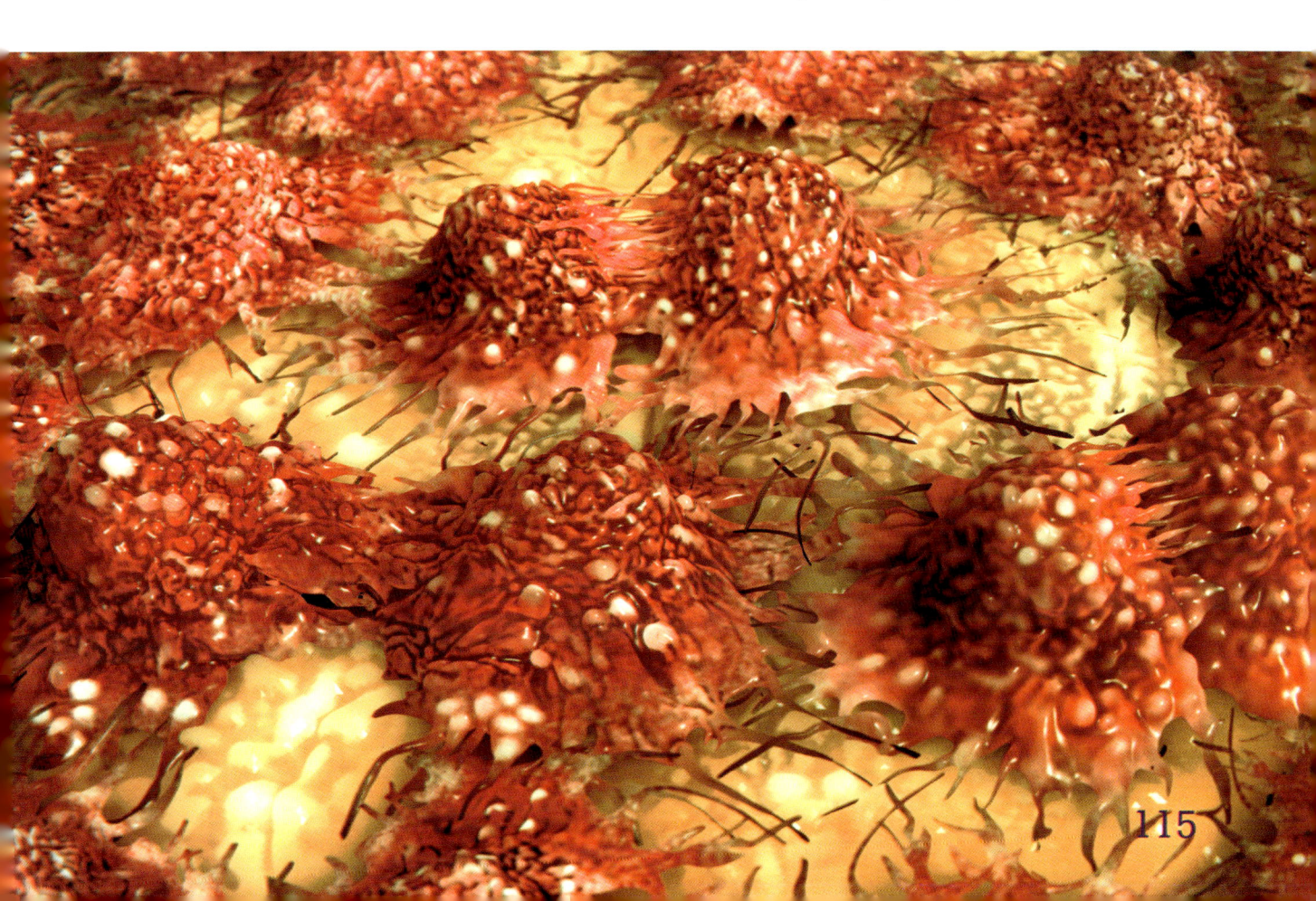

Sunshine and cancer

Sunlight is one of nature's healing remedies but too much sun is dangerous, particularly for fair-skinned people. A light tan protects fair skins from sun damage, but too much sun before a light tan has developed causes sunburn, and skin cancers can develop many years later in areas that have previously been sunburnt. Too little sun contributes to cancer too, because moderate sunlight stimulates the immune system. Also, the skin produces vitamin D in the sunshine, and vitamin D helps to prevent cancer. The solution for fair-skinned people is to stay out of strong sunlight until they have developed a light tan. They should then gradually increase their exposure and stay covered up or indoors during the hottest part of the day, especially in countries where the sun is high overhead. Dark skins are much more resistant to sun damage, but they are less efficient at producing vitamin D.

The most common types of skin cancer – squamous cell and basal cell carcinomas – only spread locally, and can be completely cured by local treatment. Less common and much more dangerous is malignant melanoma, a cancer that often develops from a mole. It too can be completely cured, but only if removed very early. Always seek medical advice about any changes in a mole, or about any skin lesion that doesn't heal.

Hormones and cancer

The reproductive cancers are all hormone-related. Hormone replacement therapy is associated with a small increase in such cancers, but the biggest risk is not from hormone medications but from hormones we eat in our food (such as dairy produce) and from excess hormones that our own bodies produce – for example, if we are overweight.

Early puberty and late menopause are associated with a higher incidence of breast cancer. Both these factors are features of the Western, high-animal-fat-and-protein, sedentary lifestyle, as is a much higher incidence of breast cancer. Dairy produce is the dietary factor of most concern because of the amount of hormones it contains.

Smoking and lung cancer

Lung cancer kills more people than any other kind of cancer. A lifetime smoker has a risk some 20-30 times higher than that of a non-smoker, and, sadly, this very common cancer has one of the lowest survival rates. Smoking is now considered to increase the risk of all cancers. Most cancers of the throat and oesophagus are directly related to cigarette smoking, and high alcohol consumption compounds the risk. Not smoking greatly lowers the risk of these and other cancers; avoiding alcohol as well is even better.

Cancer and diet

In the rich countries of the West, after lung cancer, the most common types of cancer for men are of those of the colon and the prostate. In women, breast and colon cancer are the most common. Extensive evidence links these types of cancer with over-nutrition – too many calories, and in particular too much fat. Cancers of the breast, colon, and prostate are rare in Japan, where the diet is low in fat and high in grains. Studies of Japanese people migrating to the USA, however, show that as they change to the Western diet, with its much higher intake of animal fat, they eventually develop the same cancer incidence as the local American population. There are two factors – too much of the wrong kind of food, which overloads our systems with calories and lacks other nutrients – and not enough of the right foods, the whole, unrefined plant foods with their health-promoting components: the vitamins, minerals, antioxidants, phytochemicals, and fibre.

Daily consumption of fruits and vegetables reduces the risk of cancer. These foods are rich in natural protective substances. They include vitamins, minerals and phytochemicals (special plant compounds), and they are high in fibre. A high-fibre diet reduces the transit time of food through the intestines, minimising the time available for harmful substances to irritate the lining of the colon.

The beauty of colourful fruits and vegetables

The colours themselves have powerful health-promoting properties: for example, lycopene, the red pigment in tomatoes, strawberries and other fruits, is a phytochemical with potent anti-cancer and anti-ageing properties. Lycopene first hit the headlines as a help to preventing prostate cancer, but it has many other valuable properties and probably helps to prevent all cancers. It is more easily absorbed from cooked tomatoes, especially if some oil is used. If it's made from tomatoes and it's red, it's got lycopene.

Beta-carotene, the precursor of vitamin A, is found in fresh fruits and vegetables, especially in the bright yellow and orange ones, and in dark-green leafy vegetables. It, along with vitamins C and E, is a strong antioxidant, and combats the cell damage that can lead to cancer. Scientists have observed that people who regularly eat generous amounts of fruits and vegetables have a lower incidence of cancer than those who don't. Phytochemicals such as flavonoids, carotenoids and the trace element selenium all interfere with the process of cancer initiation and help block the formation of tumours.

Among the first foods studied for their anti-cancer properties were garlic and onions. The cabbage family and the carrot family, which also includes celery, parsnip, parsley and coriander, are also known for their anti-cancer properties. Others are citrus fruits; berries; whole grains; herbs, such as mint, rosemary and sage; and soya beans. Every natural, unrefined plant food studied so far has been shown to contain health-promoting phytochemicals, with tomatoes, cherries and berries being some of the best-known.

Cancer and the animal connection

Red meat and preserved meats are particularly involved in colon and rectum cancer, and other research shows that vegetarians have a lower risk of cancer in general. Dairy produce is not as healthy as many think. Cancer incidence, especially of the reproductive cancers, is related to dairy produce. Milk and milk products contain an insulin-like growth hormone that stimulates cells to divide and grow, which is dangerous when cancer cells are present.

The World Cancer Research Fund (WCRF), in their 1997 report, *Food, Nutrition and the Prevention of Cancer*, advised choosing 'predominantly plant-based diets rich in variety of vegetables and fruits, pulses (legumes) and minimally processed foods'.

Danger signals – Seek medical advice for any of these:

Unexplained weight loss.
Unexplained change in bowel or bladder habit.
Unusual unexplained bleeding or discharge.
A thickening or lump in breast or other tissue.
Persistent difficulty in swallowing.
Persistent indigestion.
A persistent cough.
Persistent hoarseness.
An obvious change in a wart or mole.
A sore that does not heal.

By eating less fat (especially animal fat) and less refined food (especially sugar), and replacing these things with extra fresh fruits and vegetables, you can actually help to reduce your risk of cancer. An awareness of the role of positive lifestyle factors like exercise, drinking enough water and cultivating a cheerful state of mind helps you to increase the benefit. If you do these things your chances of becoming another cancer statistic are reduced: and in addition, you will feel fitter and enjoy life more.

Cancer treatment

Cancer treatment availability varies widely from place to place. Up-to-date and high-tech treatments that are widely available in the rich, developed countries may only be available in big cities in other countries – and then possibly at a price that only the rich can afford. This makes prevention all the more important. Early diagnosis is vital, too, because the earlier a cancer is diagnosed, the simpler the treatment and the better the chance of survival. So reporting unusual symptoms, especially if they persist, is essential. Of course, not all of these signs will be due to cancer: but if they are, early reporting can make the difference between life and death.

Just as there are so many types of cancer, there are also many types of treatment, and oncology is a highly specialised field. Cancer is usually a slowly-developing long-term chronic disease, and though ideally treatments would all aim at cure, this is often not possible. The aim is then to control or suppress the disease process. The main three types of treatment are:

Surgery
This is the removal, where possible, of the cancer.

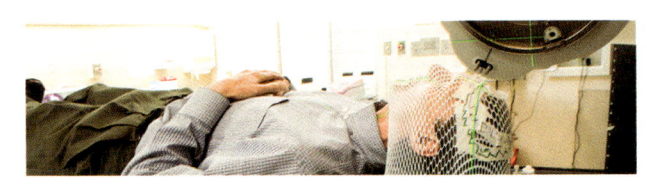

Radiotherapy
This is the use of X-rays or other radiation to kill the cancer cells, which are more sensitive and therefore more easily destroyed than normal, healthy cells.

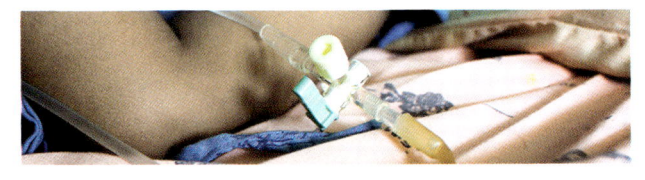

Chemotherapy
This is the use of cytotoxic (cell-poisoning) drugs which specifically attack the cancer cells and, ideally, spare all other cells.

These methods may be used alone, but often a combination of treatments is used. Cancer treatment regimes are constantly under review, and new treatments are being developed all the time, aimed at destroying or suppressing cancer cells in a variety of different ways.

Whatever the treatment, the healthy lifestyle factors are important because they will not only strengthen the body's own defences, but help the body to get the best results from the treatment.

Worldwide the seven most common cancers (56% of all cancer deaths):

- Breast 11%
- Liver 7%
- Colon 9%
- Cervix 5%
- Lung 12%
- Stomach 7%
- Prostate 6%

Ten recommendations for personal choices to reduce your risk of cancer

The World Cancer Research Fund make the following recommendations, based on their 2007 Expert Report, which contains the most comprehensive research available on cancer prevention. They emphasise diet, physical activity and weight management. Along with not smoking, these factors are the key to preventing many cancers in the UK and around the world.

1 Stay as slim as possible without becoming underweight.
Because convincing evidence shows that obesity increases the risk of breast, bowel and other cancers, control your weight, and do this by a healthy diet and regular exercise.

2 Have at least 30 minutes of physical activity a day.
Doing this will help to protect against cancer and will also help maintain a healthy weight.

3 Avoid sugary drinks and limit high-sugar, low-fibre or high-fat processed foods (junk foods).
These foods are high in calories and low in nutrients – contributing to weight gain and lowering the body's defences.

4 Eat mainly whole, unrefined plant foods.
Such foods should include a variety of fruits, vegetables, grains and pulses, because these foods contain the fibre, antioxidants and phytochemicals that protect against cancer.

5 Limit intake of red meat and avoid processed meats.
Try to steer clear of meats such as bacon, ham, salami and so on. (Better still, cut out flesh foods altogether.) Strong evidence links processed meats, especially smoked and salted meats, with bowel and stomach cancer.

120

6 If consumed at all, limit alcohol to two drinks a day for men, one for women.
Any alcohol at all increases the risk of cancer.

7 Avoid salty foods and those processed with salt.
They are associated with stomach cancer.

8 Get your vitamins and minerals from your food, not from supplements.
It is cheaper and doesn't have the danger of upsetting the balance.

9 And don't smoke!

10 Plus a special one for mothers:
Mothers, do breastfeed your babies for the first six months; it protects you against breast cancer.

11 And one more, for cancer survivors:
Follow the diet and lifestyle recommendations for cancer prevention.

If you suspect cancer, seek medical advice at once!

If you are diagnosed with cancer:

Examine your lifestyle and as far as possible follow the World Cancer Research Fund recommendations: eat a wide variety of simple, unrefined plant foods, take regular exercise, avoid as far as possible all poisons, but especially alcohol and tobacco, and cultivate an attitude of optimism and gratitude.

All these factors, especially the last one, are vitally important for strengthening the immune system to fight cancer, but in no way do they take the place of wise and skilful medical treatment. And be sure to tell your medical team about any major changes in lifestyle that you plan to make so they can be co-ordinated with your treatment.

Information in this chapter is from the World Health Organisation, World Cancer Research Fund, Cancer Research UK, and *The China Study* by Dr T. Colin Campbell, Ben Bella Books 2006.

11 Dangerous addictions

'Respectable' drugs

Alcoholism is the world's third major disease, with 2.5 million deaths annually, killing 195,000 people a year in Europe alone. All alcoholics begin as 'moderate drinkers'. Cigarette smoking kills 5 million people each year globally. Despite these frightening facts, alcohol and smoking are, more or less, socially acceptable drugs. Nevertheless, they are killers.

When we hear the word 'drugs', we tend to think of the vast illegal drug trade, which accounts for 2-5 million deaths annually worldwide. At the same time, however, we should not forget the other 'socially acceptable' or prescription drugs trade, which includes tranquillisers and sleeping tablets. The dangers surrounding the abuse of over-the-counter medicines, although they receive less public attention, are probably greater than those for the 'controlled' or illegal drugs, simply because they are more generally available.

Everyone knows that the trade in hard drugs is big business. Few are aware, however, that the business involved in prescription drugs is even bigger. The pharmaceutical industry is one of the fastest-growing in the world. Millions are spent on advertising, and the promotion of brand names to doctors has a great influence on what product will eventually be prescribed to patients. The pharmaceutical industry spends on average over twice as much on advertising as it does on the research and development of new products. In many Western countries there is one drug company representative for every eight doctors.

Around eleven million prescriptions for tranquillisers are issued annually in England alone. 'Minor' tranquillisers, such as Valium and sleeping pills, are the most common drugs on repeat prescription and taken in prolonged use. They will control the initial symptoms of anxiety, but used on their own they cannot control an emotional or spiritual problem. Used over a long period these drugs can hinder rather than help, simply because they prevent the patient discovering the root of the problem and coming to terms with the real issues he or she is facing. It has been estimated that between one third and one half of all those who take these 'minor' tranquillisers regularly each day, for three months or more, are likely to become psychologically dependent on them.

Tackling the causes

We should seriously consider tackling the stresses of everyday life by making a supreme effort to get at the cause of the situation rather than merely dealing with its symptoms.

Drugs can be used to *control* and *treat* some illnesses, and these should always be used under medical supervision. Frankly speaking, *many of the conditions for which patients consult doctors these days could be better treated in ways other than by drugs*. Many illnesses have a mental component that can be helped considerably by sympathetic understanding and an explanation of the disease process.

Worries concerning financial, social and marital problems loom large in the minds of many these days. The problems of housing and overcrowding can make tempers brittle, especially when children play up. Often a brief consultation with a general practitioner is not the best answer to the many stress-related problems that arise. One is likely to come away with a prescription for tranquilliser pills given by the doctor as a temporary measure until he can see his patient on several subsequent occasions to try to understand the underlying problem and find an answer. These may help temporarily, but it is far better to try to get help with the root cause than smother the symptoms with drugs.

Here are a few suggestions:

Be honest with yourself – don't complain of some bizarre symptom if you know that the real trouble is disharmony at home, a financial problem or some other issue.

Share the problem with a reliable relative or friend who will respect your confidence. This could well be someone other than a best friend with whom you often associate. You will be surprised how anxious people are to help, if you give them the chance and approach them sensibly.

If more professional advice is needed you might get this from your doctor, health visitor, the local minister or a social worker – depending on the particular difficulty.

If it proves impossible to resolve the situation, your doctor may then refer you to a consultant or prescribe medication. Any drugs taken should only be used under the medical supervision of one person. Otherwise confusion may result.

Finally, why not consult the Great Physician? Prayer is a two-way communication and is available free, anywhere, any time. To a believer the therapeutic value of this is profound.

What drugs do to the body

Pharynx

Cocaine constricts the arteries of the nasal passages and blocks the supply of oxygen to these delicate tissues, causing many cells to die. With time, enough cells can slough off to cause irreparable damage to the pharynx.

Vocal cords

Cigarette smoke can cause changes in the elasticity of the cord, producing changes in the voice. A multitude of malignant cancers of the respiratory system – from the mouth to the lungs – can be linked to smoking.

Lungs

For smokers, cigarette smoke destroys the cilia lining the trachea, causing bronchitis or 'smoker's cough'. Continued smoking will eventually rupture the tiny air sacs of the lungs, leading to emphysema. Talcum powder, used to cut heroin and other intravenous drugs, can clog the tiny arteries of the air sacs, causing the lungs to fill with fluid.

Pancreas

Alcohol is considered the number-one cause of pancreatitis in the United States. Its toxic effects can extensively damage the cells, which then release digestive enzymes into the surrounding tissues – in effect, digesting itself. Continued alcohol consumption can lead to gastritis, diabetes and the complete loss of pancreatic function.

Digestive system

Drugs taken by mouth, such as narcotics, can cause nausea and vomiting. Heavy use of alcohol can erode the stomach lining, cause diarrhoea, and induce massive internal bleeding. On the other hand, stimulants such as cocaine and amphetamines reduce bowel function and cause constipation.

Brain
Most abused drugs in some way modify the functions of the brain or the perceptions of the mind. Extended use of such intoxicants and stimulants can cause loss of brain tissue, decreased mental acuity, and a wide variety of psychological disorders. Over-stimulation of the brain, as with high doses of a form of cocaine known as 'crack', can lead to seizures, or even death.

Circulatory system
People who smoke have a greatly increased risk for atherosclerosis – a condition where the arteries become 'crunchy', clogged with brittle deposits of cholesterol. Nicotine, a stimulant from cigarette smoke, raises the blood pressure, which aggravates circulatory problems brought on by clogged arteries, and sometimes causes peripheral vascular disease. Aside from accidents and diabetes, this condition is the single leading cause of amputation.

Heart
Stimulants, such as cocaine and amphetamines, speed up the heart rate and raise blood pressure. Such stimulation, especially when coupled with heart disease or other cardiac insufficiency, can lead to chest pains or, in severe cases, heart attack.

Liver
Here complex molecules – some of which may be toxic – are metabolised to simpler, less harmful components. Some drugs, such as alcohol, produce toxic by-products when metabolised, and these products can cause extensive cellular damage to the liver. Dead cells are replaced with scar tissue, which over time causes the liver to become hard and fibrous – a condition known as cirrhosis. A cirrhotic liver loses its capacity to detoxify the blood, causing jaundice, fatigue, mental disorders and death.

Tobacco

People who smoke do so for a variety of reasons, mostly social and psychological, and they will have reinforced their habits over varying periods of time. The intense physical desire to smoke, in association with their range of life events and personal experiences, is what leads to their psychological addiction to tobacco. Were it not for the latter, and the medical problems that it causes, smoking really would be the pleasure that smokers claim.

Nobody sets out to become physically addicted. It is a subtle process. As the Chinese proverb has it, 'Habits are cobwebs at first, cables at last.' Medical writer Thomas McKeown hit the nail on the head when he stated: 'Our habits commonly begin as pleasures of which we have no need and end as necessities in which we have no pleasure. Nevertheless, we tend to resent the suggestion that anyone should try to change them, even on the disarming grounds that they do so for our own good. . . . It is said that the individual must be free to choose whether or not he wishes to smoke. But he is not free; with a drug of addiction the option is open only at the beginning, so that the critical decision to smoke is taken, not by consenting adults but by children below the age of consent.'[1]

Stopping smoking means that the would-be quitter has to attack the psychological and physical addictions simultaneously. Choice is part of the equation for success. Smokers have to choose not to smoke and then work through strategies that will enable them to break their habits.

Few people today can be ignorant of the ill effects of smoking. Right from their school days people have learned that smoking harms their lungs, heart, arteries, brain, kidneys, bladder, skin and eyes. They know that smoking raises blood pressure; harms the unborn baby directly by lowering birth weight and increasing disease susceptibility; speeds up the ageing process; and promotes heart disease and cancers that lead to disability and premature death.

For some people facts and statistics alone will be sufficient motivation to quit, but others will not be moved by the data concerning these diseases and conditions. Disease and death are associated with old age rather than youth. Waiting for the signs and symptoms of health problems to appear before action to quit is taken may have disastrous consequences.

A clean break

Although many smoking cessation plans advise cutting down, with a particular quit-date in mind (which may seem psychologically more bearable), the evidence suggests that it is in fact better to make a clean break.

This has been demonstrated most dramatically in studies with pregnant women who smoke. Researchers concluded that there was a direct correlation between the number of cigarettes smoked and decrease in the baby's weight. The data showed that a baby's weight decreased sharply for every cigarette the mother smoked and levelled off at a low weight around eight cigarettes a day, so just cutting down was no help. Men or women smoking even one cigarette raise their blood pressure for up to nine hours and make their lungs work harder. Making a clean break allows all the body systems to get back to something approaching normality faster.

Eliminating nicotine

The good news about quitting smoking is that the physical addiction (but not necessarily its effects) is not such a hard matter to deal with as one might suspect. In fact it will go almost as quickly as it takes the body to be rid of nicotine, usually within 36-72 hours providing the following advice is followed. Nicotine has one redeeming feature: it is soluble in water. Assuming, of course, no more nicotine is introduced to the body, the body will eliminate nicotine quite naturally via the urinary system, by sweating and during the normal course of breathing.

The process can be speeded up by drinking lots of water and by perspiring more. Extra baths or showers will help keep the skin pores open and able to work efficiently at elimination. The use of a well-wrung warm flannel mitten rub over the body extremities and torso will help to improve circulation and the elimination of the nicotine residues.

Since nicotine is a stimulant, the fact that the smoker is not getting his or her daily dose, and is eliminating residual amounts, will leave him or her feeling very tired. The first three or four days are the worst, leaving the individual emotionally drained and sometimes depressed. However, sticking to the elimination process for about ten days will bring a positive change, both physically and emotionally.

Try to avoid quick pick-me-ups. There is good reason for this, for the nicotine habit has been reinforced (both physically and psychologically) by the use of drinks containing caffeine. Caffeine has a similar molecular make-up to nicotine, so using caffeine can act as a very powerful trigger for the urge to smoke. Unless the nicotine/caffeine link is recognised it is quite common to see quitters drinking tea or coffee as if it were going out of fashion, and then wondering why they return quickly to their smoking habit. Avoiding caffeine-containing drinks for at least a couple of weeks will help to break the dependency and the psychological associations.

Recent advice to quitters, from a range of stop-smoking agencies, has included the use of nicotine replacement in the form of chewing gum or patches. While these have been popular and a psychological support, in the light of what has been said about nicotine, this may not be a wise route to take. Users of these items have frequently complained of nausea and disturbed sleep patterns. More importantly, however, this nicotine will also need to be eliminated from the body at some stage, so making a clean break really is best.

Some readers may be curious about whether the e-cigarette might be an aid to those who want to stop smoking. For those who are, the text box entitled 'What about e-cigarettes?' may be helpful.

What about e-cigarettes?

In recent years the e-cigarette has literally taken the world by storm. In the United Kingdom alone the number of users has grown from 700,000 in 2012 to a staggering 2.1 million in 2013. This number is made up mostly of regular tobacco users (60%) and former smokers, with a small number of users never having smoked anything before.

Basically the e-cigarette (also called a 'personal vapouriser' [PV] by some) consists of a battery-powered device that simulates tobacco smoking. Most of them resemble conventional cigarettes or pipes but there are an increasing number of these devices that have less conventional appearances.

Can electronic cigarettes help those who want to stop smoking?

The ingredients of the e-liquid used to create the vapour vary from brand to brand. It may or may not contain nicotine, but all brands contain a variety of other substances upon which long-term research is still to be conducted. It is this uncertainty in particular that has led leading government agencies in Britain and the US to urge caution in the use of these devices until suitable tests have been carried out. In a similar vein, the World Health Organisation (WHO) has also urged the public not to use them until a reputable national regulatory body declares them to be both safe and effective.

Do they actually aid people to stop smoking? There are questions like this, as yet unanswered, about the efficacy of the devices. There are also concerns that they may actually initiate an interest in smoking among children and youth. At this point it seems that the jury is still out on e-smoking – which is food for thought.

For further information see:
http://en.wikipedia.org/wiki/Electronic_cigarette and *www.theguardian.com/society/2014/may/05/rise-of-e-cigarettes-miracle-or-health-risk*

Willpower

'Use it or lose it' is the slogan when it comes to physical exercise. The same is true of the use of willpower. If you thought that willpower was some kind of philosophical motivational thinking inhabiting your mind, you would be wrong.

Willpower is the ability to make decisions and to see them through. To put it another way, the ability to choose. It has a physical basis. The frontal lobes of the brain are the regions responsible for such thinking. Keeping one's brain in as good a running order as possible will help in making choices and seeing them carried out. The chemistry of the brain is crucial to good mental functioning.

The brain requires one fifth of all the oxygen that is inhaled. Smoking, either directly or through passive smoking, robs the brain of the necessary oxygen and replaces large amounts of it with the exhaust gases of carbon monoxide and carbon dioxide. Not only that, smoking constricts blood vessels, thereby hindering the supply of whatever oxygen is available. The area of choice, among others, is weakened. Anything which encourages a good intake of oxygen, such as deep breathing and exercise activities, will help the brain to function at its best. The exercise enhances the circulation and enables the brain to think more efficiently.

Another important aspect of brain chemistry is its use of vitamins, minerals and trace elements. The nervous system is serviced in particular by the whole range of B vitamins, each with a specific role to play. A diet rich in these vitamins will help the brain to function well. Whole wheat, wholegrains, bran, wheatgerm, and yeast extracts (such as Marmite) will provide the optimum amounts of B vitamins as part of the regular daily diet.

Where the diet has been lacking B vitamins the deficiency can be remedied by adding these to the diet or by taking a B complex or Brewers' Yeast tablet (not the one with caffeine added!) as recommended on the manufacturer's label. (If you have been prescribed drugs by your doctor described as MAOs then avoid yeast products.)

Supplementation may be useful for people who show signs of physical stress and/or are not able to think clearly while quitting. Once the immediate need is passed, the diet should be able to meet one's normal requirements. If there is no obvious positive response to either the use of B supplements or the inclusion of B vitamin items in the diet the reason may be found in the amount of sugar used. As sugar metabolises (breaks down for use in the body) it burns B vitamins, so robbing the nervous system of its supplies. Cutting down on sugar may help to restore the vitamin B supply-line to the nervous system.

Willpower, then, has a physical basis which can be helped by exercise and careful attention to specific components in the diet. With the thinking apparatus working at its best, choices will be easier to make and to carry through, and willpower will become stronger with use.

All habits make chemical pathways using various routes through the nervous system. The advantage of this is that we do not have to keep making the same conscious choices over and over again. As we think and enact our choices the brain and the body work together. We call this co-operation a neuromuscular action. A ten-a-day smoker will go through the same (or similar) smoking operation at least 3,650 times a year, deeply engraining the smoking habit and doing it automatically year after year. Smoking is a neuromuscular habit.

When we choose to make changes, we establish a new habit pathway which produces chemical inhibitory substances at the nerve connections, junctions and terminals. The smoking habit is gradually replaced by the new non-smoking habit with its own pathways. Although habits can be changed, the old habit pathways do not go away; they lie dormant. In the event that someone who has stopped smoking decides (chooses) to smoke a cigarette, the old habit pathways are reactivated. This phenomenon accounts for the lapsing smoker smoking more the second or third time round than previously. One similar habit is superimposed, laid on top of another, and you have not one smoking habit, but two! Continually choosing not to smoke makes it increasingly unlikely that the old habit pathway will be called back into use. However, the risk of returning to smoking is there (although evermore distant), which is why it is said that ex-smokers are only one cigarette away from smoking.

Secondary habits

Neuromuscular habits vary from smoker to smoker. How the cigarette is smoked, the kind of personal rituals involved and the times and circumstances under which they are used, are collectively called the secondary habits of smoking.

To achieve success in quitting, a smoker will need to identify his or her secondary habits and devise strategies to deal with them. In identifying this cluster of habits it is likely that a number of clear patterns will emerge. Whether or not this happens, an underlying strategic principle is that all these habits require a range of small counter-habits that will help to break up the old pattern structures.

If, for example, a smoker uses the cigarette for creativity or stimulation before starting a job, or for relaxation after finishing one, it will be necessary to find some new and non-harmful way of achieving these ends. It is best not to rely on one particular counter-habit – overused it might become a new obsession! People soon become addicted to boiled sweets or other substitutes.

Sweets and dummy cigarettes can provide something for the mouth and hands to play with during the quitting period. However, if these or other items or activities are thought of as substitutes there is a negative psychology at work. The concept of 'substitution' is such that the word carries the connotation of being second best, not the real thing, and makes it easier to revert to smoking the 'real thing'.

Activities that are extrovert and distracting, keeping both the mind and body busy, especially in the early days of quitting, will help to while away the seemingly longer days. Avoiding, as far as possible, the usual meeting venues will also help to break smoking associations. Try a range of new and exciting options, but remember that the secondary habits of smoking will take longer than the physical addiction to shake off. It really is a change of lifestyle.

Weight control

One fear that keeps many people smoking is that after stopping they will put on a lot of weight. This is not an inevitable consequence, especially if measures are taken early enough. Nevertheless smoking and weight are connected.

For many people in a hurry, smoking becomes a substitute for eating, with breakfast being the most-missed meal. Smoking also acts as an appetite suppressant. When the individual stops smoking two things happen: the appetite returns and food tastes better; and people tend to eat more to satisfy the oral vacuum left by the missing cigarette. Even if no extra food is eaten there might still be a tendency to gain weight as the food is digested and utilised more efficiently.

The trick is not necessarily to eat less, but rather to eat sensibly. Diets low in fats and sugars will help the body not only to maintain its ideal weight but also to protect it against such conditions as heart disease and cancer, and for that reason are part of the recommended diet of the cancer and heart disease agencies.

The further recommendation to increase fruit and vegetable intake will help to provide the vitamins, minerals and trace elements referred to earlier. The vitamins will boost both the nervous and immune systems. Complex carbohydrates such as legumes, wholemeal pastas, brown rice, and potatoes are of major importance in weight control and provide slow-release energy for the body's needs.

There are some foods that lessen withdrawal symptoms and these are largely fruits and vegetables. Other foods increase withdrawal symptoms and are mainly animal proteins. Use of these can increase the urge to smoke. Fortunately, the fruits and vegetables, especially if eaten raw in salads, are not going to contribute to a weight problem, so can be eaten in fairly large amounts. It is not necessary to starve to control weight.

Being careful about what one eats has a number of advantages for the quitter. A selection of the right foods can take away the desire to smoke as well as provide all-round health benefits and an ideal weight. Balanced with exercise, which provides the extra oxygen, weight and fitness levels will soon contribute to a fine sense of well-being.

This sense of well-being might be sabotaged if alcohol is used. Not only does it provide 'empty calories' which may upset the weight control efforts, but it also adversely affects the frontal lobes of the brain where the willpower is located. It is important not to let down one's guard when trying to exercise willpower. It helps those trying to quit if they avoid alcohol (and places where alcohol is consumed) while involved in their smoking-cessation process.

Outside help

Surprising as it may seem, there are people who stop smoking without any major problems. While that is no consolation to those who do experience difficulties, having withdrawal symptoms or interpersonal problems is no shame either. We all differ and so do our circumstances. Some people are happy to go it alone and would prefer to emerge triumphant without any kind of help.

The statistics show that many can give up if they know that there are other people sharing their problems. To these, group quitting sessions have been a valuable source of support. However, it is not necessary to have the formal structure of a cessation programme to have a similar level of support. Besides, there might not be one around when you need it most.

Family members or friends can be either the best support or the worst of enemies when one is giving up smoking. 'Friends' who encourage us to have 'just one cigarette' can be a constant pain! With so many people now not smoking it has become easier to surround oneself with non-smokers who can give moral and practical support. Indeed, one of the main reasons for quitting may be that the individual is the only person in the work/social group still smoking. In any case, seeking the company of non-smokers during the quitting period may be of great help.

It should not be forgotten that divine help is also available. People of faith everywhere testify to the power that comes to the individual through prayer. So having a faith and being able to draw on it during what might be a time of crisis makes sound sense. Research amply demonstrates the power of prayer in overcoming problems associated with health difficulties and has been recognised as a powerful motivating and healing force by the World Health Organisation in connection with smoking cessation.

Emergency situations call for emergency reserves, so using whatever helpful resources are to hand will supply the necessary support, whether you do it individually or as part of a group. Let God do your worrying!

Stress free

People who start smoking again give stress as the number-one reason for doing so. Smoking is, however, an inappropriate response to stress. There is a false sense of security that comes from believing that a cigarette can actually relax us.

Identifying the causes of stress and devising workable strategies for dealing with them, without using cigarettes, is a must. The chapter entitled 'How to cope with stress' will help you here. Then, when the stress comes along, it can be handled appropriately. Where possible, learning specific stress-coping techniques and finding a suitable relaxation method will help to minimise the effects of stress. Add to these the dietary stress-proofing and exercise programme referred to earlier and even the hardest-craving smoker should be able to survive!

Most of the anxieties that ex-smokers experience come from anticipating situations where cigarettes would previously have been used. As these cannot always be avoided, meet these situations with a coping plan in mind. Do not panic and, whatever happens, do not find excuses for going back to smoking.

Some of the difficulties can be avoided by following some basic DOs and DON'Ts:
- Get the support of someone you can generally rely on when things get tough.
- Never offer cigarettes to anybody, not even the cigarettes you have left over.
- Do not buy or carry cigarettes for anybody else.
- Do not keep cigarettes around the house for that 'just in case' moment.
- Never light a cigarette for anybody.
- Have only non-smoking passengers in your car.
- Use only non-smoking accommodation and compartments while travelling.
- Do not give smoking equipment as gifts (ashtrays, lighters, cigarette cases, and so on).
- Put away your ashtrays.

To summarise:
- Choose not to smoke.
- Do not give in to peaks of craving. Although intense, these do not last long, but gradually space themselves out and diminish in intensity.
- Follow the dietary advice.
- Start a rewarding exercise programme, whether alone or with others. Whatever happens, keep active but don't push yourself to the point of fatigue.
- Get plenty of fresh air.
- Learn a suitable relaxation technique.
- Trust in God.
- Have regular medical checkups for peace of mind and if any symptoms related to your smoking persist.

For most people giving up smoking will be relatively easy if the above pointers are kept in mind. Your motivation for quitting is important. The more reasons for stopping that can be included in the mental list, the better. Try to encourage others not to smoke; it will reinforce your choice and give them support. Do not overdo it though: 'There is none so righteous as the newly converted!'

Alchohol

If the advertisements are to be believed, various brands of alcohol will enhance the user's appeal to the opposite sex, change their social strata and status, and add glamour to their otherwise colourless lives. Whatever we may think about its use, alcohol is commonly used to celebrate the arrival of the newborn child to the world, recognise particular social landmarks along life's way, and show respect for the deceased. Besides all that, most people drink alcohol for the sheer 'pleasure' of it.

The use of alcohol has a dark side, however; one that is defined in the World Health Organisation's authoritative *Global Status Report on Alcohol and Health 2014* on page xiii: 'Alcohol is a psychoactive substance with dependence-producing properties that has been widely used in many cultures for centuries. The harmful use of alcohol causes a large disease, social and economic burden in societies.'

What is there about this substance that wields so much power and has such a wide-ranging effect? There are a number of alcohol solutions which are used in domestic, commercial or manufacturing processes. The one that is used as a drink is *ethyl alcohol* (C_2H_5OH) and, depending on the drink used, it is found in varying concentrations. It is made either by fermentation (as in beer) or by distillation (as in whisky). The ethyl alcohol produced is a central-nervous-system depressant, contrary to the opinion of many that alcohol is a stimulant. When ethyl alcohol is drunk the body breaks it down (as part of the digestive process) first into *acetaldehyde*, then *acetate*, and finally into the waste products of *carbon dioxide* (CO_2) and *water* (H_2O). It takes approximately one hour to load the system with alcohol, and about 10-12 hours for it to be broken down into CO_2 and H_2O and eliminated from the body by exhalation and urination (passing water).

The calories (or units of energy) provided by alcohol ingestion are often referred to as 'empty calories' in that they do not provide any nutritional value to the body. They are stored in the body fat, hence the joking reference to beer-drinker's belly.

Effects of alcohol

It is socially acceptable to drink alcohol in most countries worldwide, the exceptions being those countries which see alcohol use as contrary to the prevailing religious belief. While it may be a matter of personal choice and taste to drink alcohol, we should be aware that it does have adverse effects. These occur literally from the moment of use and, as might be expected, increase with the amount and/or particular alcoholic drink chosen. Since many of the changes that take place are incremental and are not noticed immediately, the continued use of alcohol may lead to a false sense of security in matters regarding health risks.

The effects of alcohol as it goes through the body include the following:

Mouth
An increasing thickening of the tissues that line the mouth; a gradual loss of taste, compensated for by an increase in condiment use, particularly pepper and mustard; such changes to the tissues may predispose to cancers of the mouth.

Pancreas
The cells of the pancreas become irritated, swell, and bleed (haemorrhagic pancreatitis). The flow of digestive enzymes is blocked and once the cells are damaged or destroyed diabetes will set in.

Stomach and intestines
Some degree of alcoholic gastritis is found in around 30% of alcohol users to some degree. It causes stomach and duodenal ulcers, which heal when alcohol is not used.

Ninety-five percent of the alcohol used is absorbed into the bloodstream through the stomach and intestines, which interferes with nutrition, affecting the digestion, storage, use and excretion of nutrients: in particular, thiamine (B1), B12, folic acid, fat, and some amino acids. It can also cause the stomach lining to shrink.

Heart
Alcohol inflames and damages heart muscle (cardiomyopathy), leads to fatty degeneration, and (along with the effect on the liver) causes an increased risk of atherosclerosis (hardening of the arteries).

Circulatory system
The superficial blood vessels dilate, causing the individual to feel warm while actually experiencing heat loss, which leads to a chilling of the body.

Alcohol slows down the circulation and the action of the white blood cells, thus delaying our resistance to infection. This greatly increases the susceptibility of alcohol users to various diseases.

Alcohol causes the red blood cells to clump together, thereby increasing the risk of blood clotting, and inhibiting oxygen transportation to the tissues (anaemia).

Liver
When these tissue cells are inflamed they block the tiny canals to the small intestine, bile is not filtered properly and jaundice results.

Tissue cells are destroyed with each drink taken, leading to cirrhosis of the liver (a condition eight times more common in the alcohol-dependent), and fatty degeneration of the tissue.

Nutritional deficiencies are also experienced due to the person taking alcohol in preference to nourishing food.

Sex glands and womb
Alcohol causes swelling of the prostate gland, and interferes with sexual performance.

1-2 units (see chart) daily during the first three months of pregnancy may lead to spontaneous abortion.

10+ units daily during pregnancy may result in *Foetal Alcohol Syndrome* (FAS) in which physical injury is caused to the developing foetus.

Kidneys and bladder
Alcohol increases fluid loss and extra water is expelled, causing the bladder to become inflamed, making it difficult to stretch and accommodate the extra fluid.

Brain and spinal cord
We have already noted that alcohol is a depressant, but it also has anaesthetic and analgesic (pain-relieving) properties.

Alcohol causes a gradual destruction of the cells of the cortex of the brain (the outer area) with shrinkage of the surface of the brain. Cells lost are never renewed.

It also causes loss of control and slows reflex actions. For example, approximately 2 cocktails, which is half a drop of alcohol per thousand drops of blood (0.05%), slows reflexes by 10%.

Alcohol has an affinity for nerve cells with a high lipid (fat) content, so higher concentrations of alcohol are found in nervous tissue.

Many of the above changes (which are by no means exhaustively described) occur even in the presence of adequate nutrition and are accelerated where good nutrition is lacking.

It has been widely publicised that a little alcohol is good for the heart. Strictly speaking this is unlikely to be true. The research that led to this media conclusion was the British Regional Heart Study,[2] in which abstainers' heart conditions were compared with those of moderate and heavy drinkers. The results appeared to show that the moderate drinkers had better heart health than either abstainers or heavy drinkers.

What was not known at the time was that the abstainers studied were people who had been told to quit drinking because of an existing heart condition. The results might have been quite different if lifetime abstainers had been used in the study. Although an abstaining person is not necessarily a fit person, moderate drinkers may be careful in other aspects of their health. The author of the study says that, on the basis of the report, no one should start drinking to protect their heart as the amount of alcohol said to confer benefit would still harm the liver and the brain. Other studies have shown that it was not necessarily alcohol that protected, but rather an ingredient (flavonoid) found in the skin of red grapes (and, incidentally, in the skins of all red fruits and vegetables).

Blood alcohol levels and effects

Blood alcohol concentration levels cause measurable changes in behaviour, reactions and responses, which will usually increase with the quantity of alcohol imbibed; however, persons not used to drinking alcohol may experience similar effects at much lower levels.

50mg/100ml A loosening of inhibitions, impaired judgement and increased cheerfulness. This state is often mistakenly thought to arise from a stimulant effect of alcohol. It is produced by 1½ pints of beer, 3 whiskies, or a half-bottle of wine.

150mg/100ml A loss of self-control, exuberance or quarrelsomeness, and slurred speech, caused by 5 pints of beer, 10 whiskies, or 1 litre of wine.

400mg/100ml Sleepiness, coma, oblivion. This would be induced by ¾ bottle of spirits, and so on. This and the following in any amounts above those already indicated:
500mg/100ml Death possible.
600mg/100ml Death virtually assured.

Cause and effect

The following amounts of alcohol, per 100ml of blood, are likely to have effects which include:

30mg/100ml The increased risk of an accident. This results from drinking 1 pint of beer, 2 glasses of wine or a double whisky.

80mg/100ml The loss of one's driving licence in most countries if caught driving under the influence of this much alcohol. An intake of 2½ pints of beer, 5 whiskies, or 5 glasses of wine would put one in this state.

200mg/100ml Double vision, a staggering walk and loss of memory – this would be achieved through 6 pints of beer, ½ bottle of spirits, or 2 bottles of wine.

1 unit
(8g alcohol)

1 shot spirits   1 small wine   ½ pint beer

138

Clearly, some people may be able to consume larger volumes of alcohol than indicated above without apparently displaying the corresponding effects. This is because their drinking pattern has become established at higher levels (a process known as toleration), which allows them to use more alcohol before the same effects are observed. This is a dangerous practice, especially if deliberately entered into, because of the serious physical effects of the alcohol. In the light of the damage sustained there is really no such thing as sensible drinking.

Acute and chronic effects of alcohol

The effects of alcohol on society can be seen in the opening statistics of this chapter. The following effects, while having some overlap, are classified as being acute or chronic:

Acute effects include drunkenness, crime, drinking and driving, hooliganism, and family violence. Alcohol is reckoned to be a factor in 1 in 3 child cruelty cases, and 50% of physical abuse against women is alcohol-related. In one UK study, 1 in 3 women attending a women's aid hostel claimed that violence occurred regularly when their husbands were drunk.

Chronic effects include alcohol dependence, physical and mental illnesses, social problems, unemployment and suicide. These effects also carry over into the lives of family members, friends and communities.

Recovering from alcohol dependency

Some people's personal circumstances are so depressing as to be overwhelming, and these factors need to be addressed if the individual is to benefit long-term. Alcohol dependency should be seen as part of a wider lifestyle picture, and often includes other addictions.

A first step in dealing with any problem is to acknowledge that it exists, and then outline steps to deal with it.

Once the person with the dependency has recognised his or her problem they can be encouraged to find the motivation to change their harmful behaviour and seek treatment and help. In fact, at all stages in the process of recovery the individual's motivation needs to be supported.

Depending on the severity of the problem, clinical help may be necessary and a long-term course of treatment outlined. Individuals should carefully follow the instructions for immediate treatment and any subsequent steps that need to be taken. They will need to be surrounded with the necessary emotional and spiritual support that will enable them to gain strength in their decision and maintenance of a changed lifestyle. Practical support may also be necessary for some individuals until they are fully able to play their part at various levels of involvement in the home and work environment.

Sadly, some of the physical damage done may not be repaired, but a healthy lifestyle may offset any further deterioration in the person's condition. Sobriety can be maintained if the motivation and support is, and remains, strong. Keeping clear of drinking opportunities and cultivating the friendship of non-drinkers will help to provide the conditions for the individual to flourish. This may be achieved best in an accepting faith community where the spiritual input adds an extra dimension of support. The World Health Organisation recognises that spiritual motivation for health behaviour change is potent and more long-lasting than many other motivations.

The advertisements tell us nothing of the problems listed above. We should not be fooled by the superficial glamour portrayed in them. Many millions of people worldwide enjoy the things that the adverts picture, but without the use of alcohol. Indeed, without the alcohol many enjoy these things even more by having real quality of life.

[1] Thomas McKeown, *The Role of Medicine: Dream, Mirage or Nemesis?* (Princeton University Press, 1979), pp. 124, 125
[2] Editorial (1991), 'Heart Disease and Drink – the health message remains clear', *Alcohol Alert*, Nov/Dec, page 3

12 Coping with allergies

Who among us does not enjoy the pleasure of a walk in the country when the air is heavy with the smell of new-mown hay and bees buzz from flower to flower collecting the precious pollen to make into golden honey? Or the sight of a long-haired cat purring contentedly in front of a blazing fire, or the gastronomic delights of strawberries and cream?

For some people, however, these spell nothing but misery in the form of running eyes, sneezing and wheezing, and perhaps even an itchy skin rash. The common factor which accounts for each of these unpleasant reactions can be summed up in a single word . . . **allergies!**

An allergy can be defined most simply as a *hypersensitivity to various substances which would normally be harmless to the average person*. It can take various forms and can involve a bewildering range of possible stimuli. When we consider all the stories about supposed allergies – some bizarre and even amusing – we realise that there may be a tendency to blame allergies for more than we should. Modern research has shown, however, that allergic responses are due to very well-defined mechanisms. These involve a) particular chemical stimuli or antigens; b) antibodies or chemical substances produced by the individual to counteract the antigens; and c) the activities of certain cells in the body which release chemicals producing the inflammatory features of the allergic reaction. There is nothing vague or imprecise about an allergy.

If genuine, it is a reaction to a specific substance to which the individual has unpredictably become sensitised, and it is likely that the symptoms will appear each time he or she is exposed to that stimulus.

Exposure to sensitising agents can be by a variety of routes.

Inhalation of airborne allergens – such as pollens – may give rise to respiratory forms of allergy such as hay fever and asthma. Ingestion may cause food allergies and rashes, and contact with skin can produce dermatitis. The symptoms, whether sneezing, wheezing, or itching, are due to inflammation at the site of entry of the allergen into the body, although once absorbed, the reaction may result in more general symptoms.

Some of the most sudden and serious allergic reactions occur when the sensitising agent is introduced directly into the circulation, as with bee stings or following the injection of certain drugs to which the individual may have become sensitised by previous medication. We should remember, however, that the development of a specific allergy is very much an individual peculiarity, and that most people similarly exposed will have no problems at all.

The range of substances to which we may become allergic is enormous, and many of these will be common items present in our food or our physical environments in the home, at our work, or in our leisure activities. Whether we develop symptoms of allergy or not is largely a matter of chance, although certain individuals appear to have a particular inherited predisposition to allergic conditions such as hay fever and asthma. Such people, known as 'atopic' subjects, may also have a tendency to eczema, a skin rash which may take a variety of forms and appear for the first time in infancy or later in childhood. These individuals produce specific antibodies known as 'reagins' in response to a variety of allergens, and this phenomenon can be demonstrated by the doctor when using skin tests, or by more specialised and expensive laboratory methods. The same tests can be carried out for food allergies but normally have no relevance to the incidence of eczema.

Common food allergens include dairy products, eggs, various nuts, shellfish and strawberries. The symptoms that follow their ingestion may take the form of a swelling of the lips or mouth, a stomach upset, an itchy rash or 'hives', urticaria ('nettle rash') or even large weals. These symptoms will appear within a short time of eating certain allergens, and will usually persist for several hours unless relieved by appropriate medication. Similar allergic reactions can occur in some individuals who develop intolerance to the colouring agents and preservatives used in the preparation of many foods.

Respiratory allergies, due to inhaled allergens, are most frequent in the pollen season, and the first symptoms will appear in the early summer months when the sufferers are troubled by sneezing, running eyes, and perhaps by bronchospasms and wheezing. The severity of these symptoms often parallels the 'pollen count', which may be forecast in your daily newspaper, or during the radio or television weather reports. This gives us an indication of the amount of various plant pollens in the air. House dust mites – tiny microscopic creatures in bedding and house dust – are also an allergic stimulus for many patients with respiratory allergies.

Dermatitis or eczema can result from skin contact with sensitising agents. Itching eczema will develop at the site of actual contact, and a careful history of the appearance of symptoms and the distribution of the rash may provide a strong clue as to the agent responsible. Allergies to rubber, chemicals, nickel, certain plants, animal dander (see box), and even to wool fat (lanolin) in cold creams, are not uncommon. Modern dermatology clinics provide facilities for the investigation of contact dermatitis caused by the vast number of allergens in our environment, and suspicions can be scientifically confirmed by patch testing (see box).

Animal dander

All warm-blooded animals shed tiny flakes from their skin, fur or feathers. This is called animal dander, and is like dandruff from humans but more difficult to see.

Patch tests

The patch test is a method used to see if a particular skin reaction is caused by exposure to a specific chemical or substance. A small amount of the suspected chemical or substance is applied to special metal discs, which are then taped to the patient's skin for 48 hours and regularly checked for possible reactions. *www.nhs.uk*

Dealing with allergies

As it is not practical to regulate one's life to avoid sensitisation, it will be more helpful to consider how one can deal with allergies which actually develop.

Identification of the allergen. The most useful clue to the identification of the sensitising substance may be provided by a detailed history. The individual may be able to link the onset of symptoms to a particular time, environment, or set of circumstances. The presenting features will probably indicate whether the allergen is in the air, in the diet, or in contact with the skin. Such suspicions can often be confirmed by specific tests, which a doctor can carry out. Food allergies or reactions to food additives may be identified by using 'elimination diets' in which the suspected item is excluded for a period of several weeks to determine whether the symptoms are alleviated. Skin allergies can similarly be confirmed by patch testing.

If the allergen can be identified with certainty it may be possible to avoid further exposure to that substance. This may merely entail minor adjustments, such as the avoidance of a particular cosmetic or plant, the substitution of latex gloves for rubber ones, or the elimination of a particular item from the diet. In some situations, however, it may be necessary to make more radical changes in one's employment or lifestyle to eliminate further contact with the allergen.

Hyposensitisation. If the allergen cannot be avoided completely it may be possible to make an individual less sensitive to it by a process known as desensitisation. This is used by doctors particularly for the treatment of hay fever and can be of considerable benefit. The patient is given a series of injections of minute quantities of the antigen and over a period of several weeks he or she will develop a tolerance to it, and be able to survive the effects of the pollen season with few or no symptoms. Such treatment must be given under strict medical supervision. Similar hyposensitisation techniques may occasionally be used for other allergens, such as bee or wasp stings and certain life-saving drugs to which the patient may have become allergic.

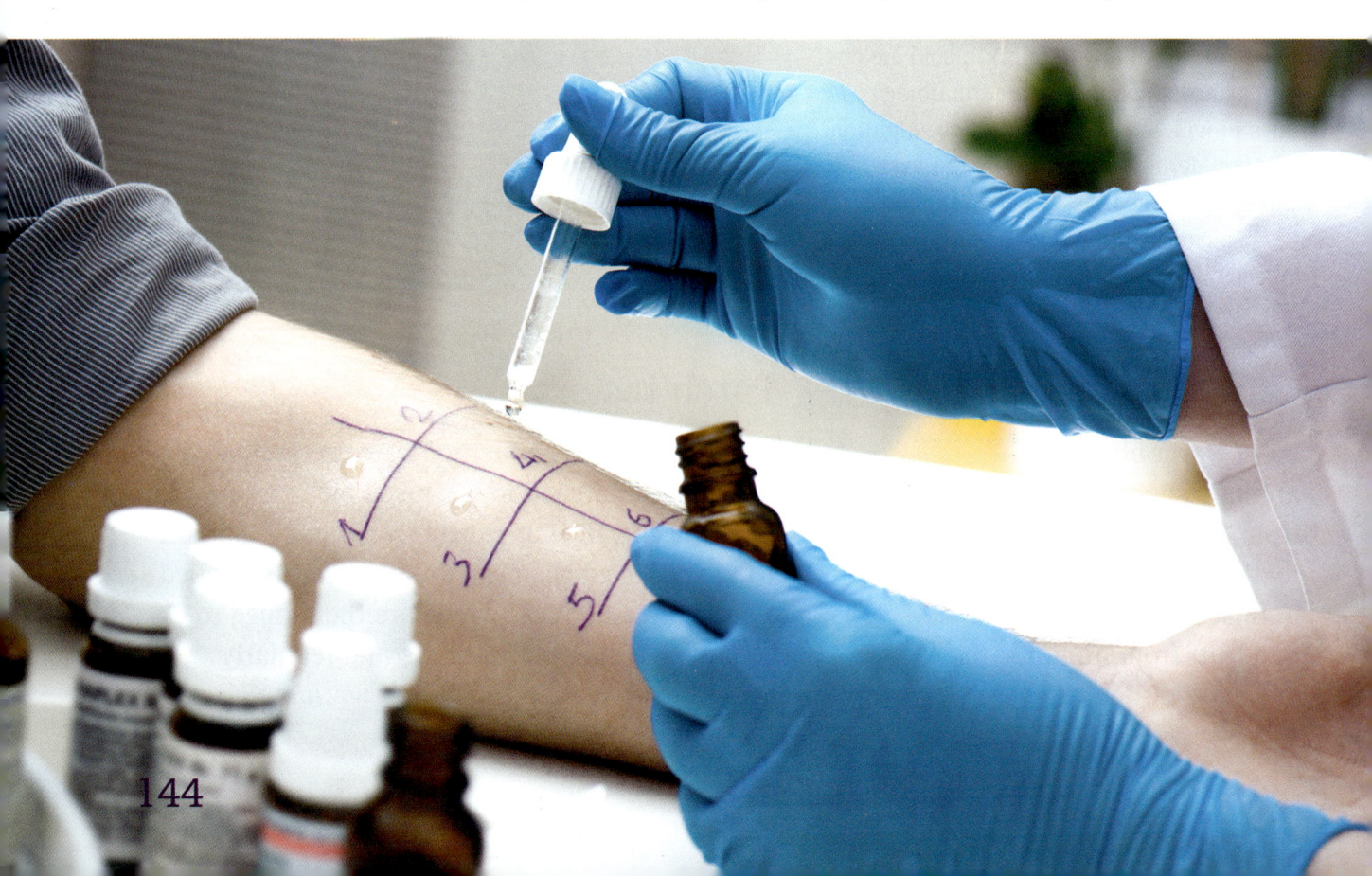

Drug treatment for allergies.

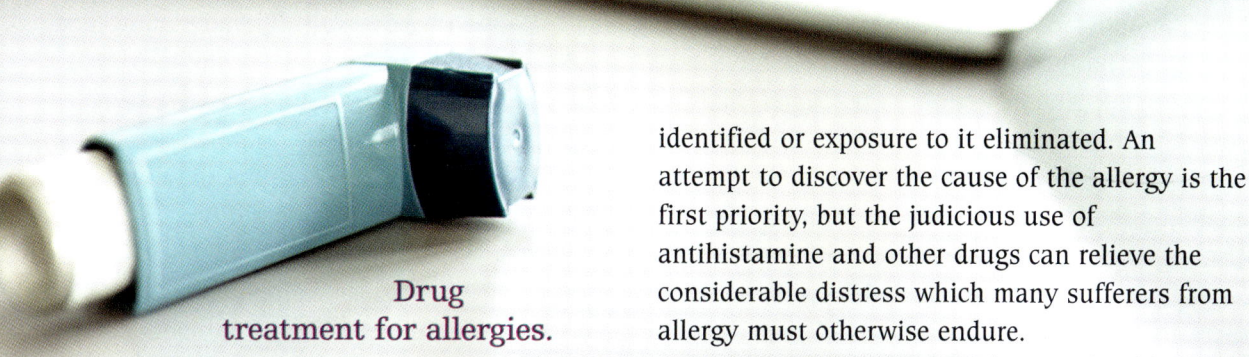

We have seen that the symptoms of allergy are due to inflammation, triggered off by the reaction between the antigen and the corresponding antibody or sensitised cells in the individual. This process releases chemicals such as histamine and other agents that cause inflammation in the tissues. The allergic symptoms can thus be relieved by the use of drugs that will neutralise these substances. A very large range of 'antihistamine' drugs is now available to effectively relieve the distress of the allergic patient. These will be helpful whether the symptoms are in the respiratory system, gastro-intestinal tract, or skin, and are an invaluable form of treatment.

Other drugs, such as cromoglycate, have been used similarly for the relief of allergic asthma in children and to counter some food allergies. The most serious reactions – such as severe bronchospasm and certain sting or drug reactions – may require emergency treatment with adrenaline or corticosteroid drugs to relieve the more acute symptoms, which may be life-threatening.

Drug treatment is of greatest value in suppressing the symptoms of allergy in those situations where the allergen cannot be identified or exposure to it eliminated. An attempt to discover the cause of the allergy is the first priority, but the judicious use of antihistamine and other drugs can relieve the considerable distress which many sufferers from allergy must otherwise endure.

Modern medicine has made considerable advances in the understanding of allergic conditions, and the provision of effective treatment for those who require it. This is important because a growing number of people around the world are suffering from some form of allergy.

> A very large range of 'antihistamine' drugs is now available which can effectively relieve the distress of the allergic patient.

Food allergies and sensitivities

Allergies are becoming much more common. According to the *World Allergy Organisation Journal*, worldwide there are at least 300 million people who suffer from asthma, 200 to 250 million who experience food allergies and 400 million with rhinitis. In addition to which, an estimated 10% of the global population suffer from drug-related allergies.[1]

An allergy is a hypersensitivity of the immune system to a foreign substance, such as pollen, house dust or particular foods, which are harmless to non-allergic people. The over-reactive immune system treats these normally harmless substances as invaders, going into emergency mode with the well-known allergic responses of wheezing (asthma), running nose (allergic rhinitis or hay fever), and skin problems (eczema, urticaria or nettle rash) and, in extreme cases, anaphylactic shock – a very dangerous, potentially fatal condition. Some people have a much greater tendency to these reactions than others, and their condition is known as atopy. Most cases of atopy involve many factors, including foods, but the term 'food allergy' is also used very widely for all sorts of reactions to foods, many of which are not allergies at all. For these the term 'food sensitivity' is better.

Both true food allergies and other food sensitivities are much more common now than they were twenty or thirty years ago. This is especially so with nut allergy, particularly peanut allergy, where a potentially fatal reaction to this normally harmless legume can come on within minutes. Unfortunately such severe reactions are much more common than they were.

Why is this so? Many people now have unstable immune systems that overreact, like a burglar alarm set to call the police when burglars enter, but which in fact goes off when a spider walks past. Instead of producing a few drops of fluid to flush out some pollen grains, these over-reactive immune systems produce a torrent of hay fever or a severe attack of wheezing. Research is needed to find out why so many people's immune systems are so sensitive. Theories range from immune system overload due to the vast number of foreign chemicals to which we are exposed now, to immune system underactivity, due to our over-hygienic environment. Another possible cause is that immunisation programmes have wiped out the childhood illnesses that helped to build healthy immune responses in the past. Probably all these factors play a part, but the fact is that we don't really know.

Although we do not fully understand food allergies and sensitivities, we do know that improving general health, lifestyle and environment can greatly diminish, if not actually completely eliminate, many of these problems. Smoke-free air for asthma sufferers is an obvious example; pollen-free air for hay fever sufferers is another. What is less well known is that asthmatics and other atopic sufferers can be helped very much by changing their diet. The same is true for those who find that specific food sensitivities cause problems as diverse as digestive upsets, sinusitis, chronic fatigue, nerve-related conditions and even arthritis.

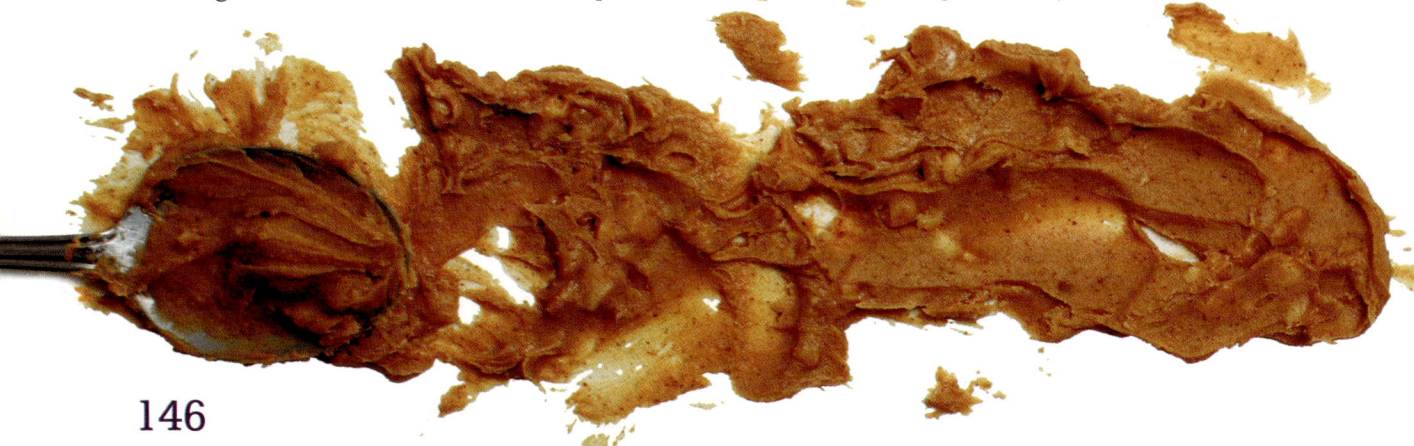

Frequently used foods are the most likely culprits – such well-trusted staples as milk, bread, chocolate and even orange juice. In the West most people have grown up to look on milk as almost the ideal form of nutrition, but it can cause major problems. Actually, as many as 90% of adults worldwide lack the enzymes needed to digest cow's milk. Milk production methods have also changed a lot in recent decades, as has the food industry. With milk in some form added to almost every processed food you can think of, many people are getting milk overload. Milk sensitivity contributes to the truly allergic (atopic) problems and also to many ear, nose and throat conditions, as well as a great many bowel disorders. Another problem food seems to be wheat. It is another frequently eaten food and many people now eat less of other cereals, such as oats, rye, barley, or rice, to balance it. It's as if the body finally gets wheat overload and goes on strike. There are now very few varieties of wheat grown, and this may well add to the problems. It's interesting that in the UK around one in every hundred people suffer from coeliac disease and have a severe gluten (wheat protein) intolerance, but many more people than that are buying expensive gluten-free products. Most of these people seem to have jumped on the gluten-free bandwagon, because they think they may be intolerant or as a precaution in case they might be. A good plan would be for them to look very carefully at their whole lifestyle as well as their diet, because there could be many other reasons for their problems.

Another problem group is the methyl xanthenes – they're in tea, coffee, chocolate and cola – another type of substance that many people use daily or more often.

Such foods increase the tendency to true allergic or atopic reactions, but acute reactions are often triggered by other less frequently used items which are usually fairly easy to recognise, such as seafood, mushrooms, specific fruits – strawberry is a well-known one – and of course the notorious peanut. Sometimes a particular combination of foods, environmental factors and mental state is necessary to trigger such reactions, which makes detection much more difficult.

So what should one do? Those who have experienced severe reactions should of course be under medical care, avoid the obvious causes and have medication for emergency use. They should continue this regime but also start lifestyle programmes to stabilise and strengthen their immune systems. Such programmes include exercise and stress control as well as a healthy diet. Those with less serious problems will benefit from such programmes too, and it's well worth trying a simple elimination diet to find out what their main triggers are.

As milk is the commonest problem food, the first step would be to eliminate it and all its by-products as completely as possible from the diet, preferably for a few weeks. If that works, try a 'challenge' – a serving of dairy produce. If the sneezing, bowel cramps or other symptoms recur, the best plan is to avoid all dairy produce for two or three months. After that many people find they can tolerate it occasionally, sometimes even regularly. The same can be done with wheat, methyl xanthenes and whatever food you suspect. If you are really keen, you can try eliminating dairy, wheat, chocolate, etc, all at the same time, then reintroduce them gradually, one by one, to see which ones cause problems.

Eliminating irritating foods is not the whole story, however. They need to be replaced by a wide variety of whole and healthy foods. Base your diet around unrefined starches, add plenty of fruits and vegetables, and smaller helpings of foods made from beans, nuts (if you're not allergic to them) and seeds. Eat a wide variety of foods from day to day, but a small variety at any one meal. Avoid eating between meals or late at night. Exercise is very important too, as is avoiding poisons. Cultivating a peaceful and contented frame of mind may be the most important remedy of all.

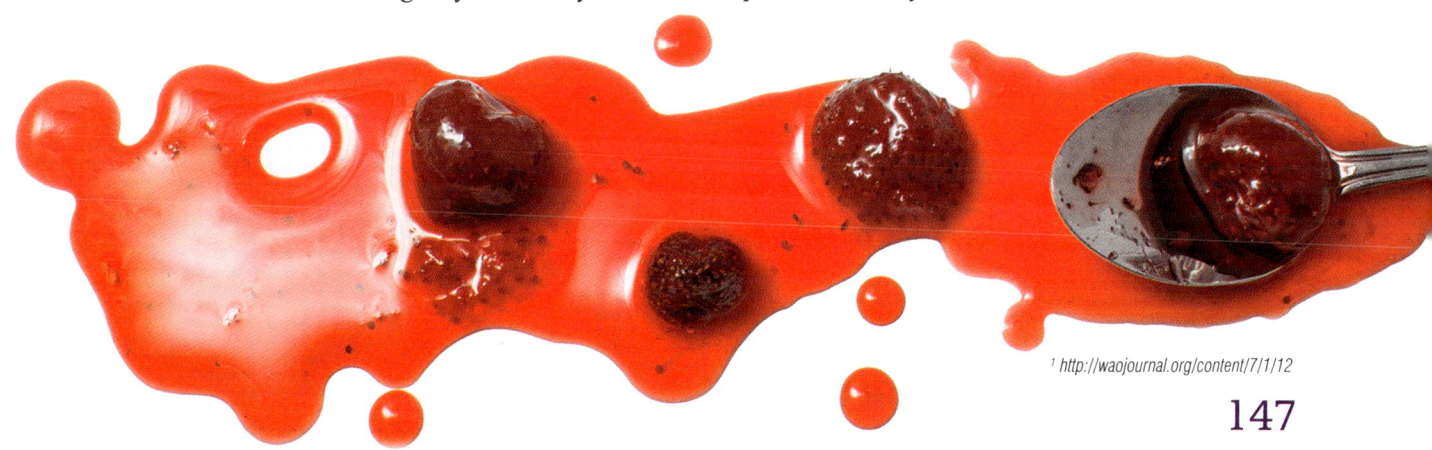

[1] http://waojournal.org/content/7/1/12

13 Benefits of belief

A professor announced to a brand-new class of medical students: 'I have good news and bad news: The good news is that half of the material you learn in medical school will survive all scrutiny and investigation. It will be enduring. The other half of what we teach you, however, will be proven incorrect. The bad news is we have no way of knowing which half is which!'

In today's world it's sometimes difficult to know what to believe about much of the information we're 'fed'! One day we read that drinking alcohol is harmful. The next week other reports indicate that it's protective of good health. Chocolate is fattening, right? Wait a minute – now a research group has reported that it actually helps people lose weight. Coffee is harmful, we've been told. But then we learn that in a significant study those who drank large amounts of coffee lived longer! And one week a major tech company introduces another time-saving, 'must have' device; the next week media report those claims as based on unreliable analyses.

In what or whom can we truly believe? Sometimes determining the answer to this question is tough! Yet, we all believe in something. The greatest sceptics have their beliefs too, even if it's the belief that no one can be trusted. The survival of all humans is based on beliefs of some kind. Belief is essential to human existence and organisation.

Power of belief

One day a physician was examining a patient who complained about a myriad of symptoms, unrelated to any known syndrome or disease complex. The patient told the doctor that perhaps an evil spell had been cast on him and was making him ill. The doctor then took two small glass tubes and filled one with hydrogen peroxide and the other with water. The patient didn't know the two liquids were different. The physician then drew a small amount of blood from the patient and put a few drops into the tube with the hydrogen peroxide. Naturally, there was an immediate reaction of effervescence, and the doctor knowingly nodded. 'Ah-ha,' he said, 'you will benefit from this.' He then gave the patient a saline injection and told him to wait in the waiting room.

After a short time the doctor called the patient back into his office and again drew a small amount of blood, this time putting a few drops into the tube containing plain water. As expected, it mixed without any reaction. The doctor told the patient that the evil spell had been broken, and the patient left feeling immensely better. The story goes that the patient told all his friends about how he had been healed, and many of them came to the doctor wanting the same treatment!

As this story demonstrates, there is tremendous power in belief. For many a peddler of 'quack medicine', this phenomenon is a mighty source of revenue. 'Unscrupulous' salespersons can sometimes create a false need in the minds of their targets. They then sell herbal concoctions, non-essential mineral supplements, nutraceuticals (fortified foods or supplements), special diets, and magnetic or electrical cures mediated through empty black boxes or mild shock-emitting equipment. They are trading on what can be called the 'gullibility factor'. For those who are healthy, the only cost is some money, from which they are soon parted. In a situation in which something such as cancer is involved, sometimes the delay before undertaking more traditional treatment leads to a deadly outcome, as well as the wasting of limited and precious resources on worthless 'cure-alls'. It's important to place our belief and trust in that which is reliable and not on such unproven methods.

Belief – or faith, within a religious setting – has been shown to have statistically significant benefits that exceed the placebo effect. When the religious experience of Americans who reached the age of 100 was studied, researchers found that religiosity significantly enhanced health. Although many questions are still unanswered, the benefits of trust in God result from more than simply attending religious services.[1]

A study comparing mortality rates between secular and religious kibbutzim (collective agricultural communities in Israel) found a decreased mortality rate over a 15-year follow-up in the religious group. The age-adjusted risk of premature death of members of the secular kibbutz was 1.8 times higher for males and 2.7 times higher for females when compared with the religious kibbutz.[2]

A study of African-Americans found that those who engaged in organised religious activities had improved health and life satisfaction.[3] Duke University researcher C. G. Ellison found that a lack of religious affiliation increases the risk of depression in African-Americans.[4]

A connection between social relationships and survival has been documented in several studies. C. J. Schoenbach, et al. have documented this effect, particularly among white males.[5]

149

Improved quality of life

One of the most consistent findings across all racial groups is that spirituality profoundly improves the quality of life. Ellison describes these significant benefits, brought about by exercising faith:[6]

- Religious attendance and private devotion strengthen a person's religious belief system.
- Strong religious systems, when accompanied by a high level of religious certainty, have a substantial and positive influence on well-being.
- Individuals with strong religious faith report higher levels of life satisfaction, greater personal happiness, and fewer negative psychosocial consequences of traumatic life events.

Spirituality not only helps believers but also benefits the nonbelievers in their community. Research has found that communities gain health benefits when they have higher numbers of adherents to faiths that emphasise implicit obedience to God and His standards of conduct.[7] The reason that nonbelievers are benefited as well is likely due to the fact that their social norms favour conformity to the more healthful lifestyle embraced by their religious neighbours.

Religious people – particularly adolescents from religious homes who frequently attend religious services, pray, and read Scripture – have fewer problems with alcohol, tobacco, or other drugs than do their nonreligious peers.[8]

Religion was also positively associated with emotionally healthful values and socially accepted behaviours, such as tutoring or other volunteer activities often promoted by religious organisations.[9]

Harold G. Koenig, MD, discusses the findings of Idler and Kasl. These researchers noted a connection between healthier emotional lives and closer social ties among religiously active people, which often resulted in lower levels of disability. The increased physical activity associated with leisure and social activities did not fully account for the increased benefits in these people's lifestyles, and the authors concluded: 'A significant effect of religiousness remains even after social activities have been considered.'[10]

Thus, we find that belief in a loving God produces a very positive and powerful health-promoting state of mind. There is nothing more reassuring than the peace and satisfaction experienced by those who place their lives in the hands of a loving God and who are aware of His love for them. This brings health, happiness, and a sense of purpose. As the Bible says, 'Those who love your instructions have great peace and do not stumble' (Psalm 119:165, NLT).

Stress issues

Belief in God may also be associated with reduction in stress, depression, and loneliness. A 1990 Gallup poll revealed that more than 36 percent of Americans live with chronic feelings of loneliness. According to a Princeton University Research Associates survey, at least two thirds of Americans feel stressed at least once a week. Stress, loneliness, and related depression can have serious consequences. Between 75 and 90 percent of all doctor visits contain components relating to stress.[11]

Medical science has discovered that when you feel stressed as a result of facing challenges, the negative emotions trigger the release of certain hormones that stimulate the nervous system in such a way as to put stress on the various organs of the body. If these organs are subjected to stress over long periods of time, they become weakened. Once weakened, they are more susceptible to a variety of disease processes. The order and intensity with which organs are affected depend upon the person's heredity, constitution, environment, and lifestyle. For example:

- Stress may cause the release of adrenaline, making the heart beat more rapidly and powerfully. Such stress can cause one to suffer from heart palpitations (unpleasant awareness of heartbeat).
- When stress hormones cause the blood vessels to constrict, they may augment the effects of hypertension and cause diminished peripheral vascular flow, leading to cold hands and feet.
- Stress may induce shallow and rapid breathing with bronchial dilation, which causes hyperventilation.
- Stress results in diversion of the blood supply away from the digestive system, possibly affecting digestive processes.
- Stress induces a state of increased clotting of the blood; though protective in some circumstances, it could have detrimental effects in others.
- Chronic stressful conditions may increase perspiration, leading to unpleasant dampness.
- Stress causes an increase in blood glucose (to serve as a rapid source of energy); in those predisposed to diabetes, chronic stress may lead to the hastening of the onset or exacerbation of diabetes mellitus.

- Stress may cause alterations in gastrointestinal and urinary functions. Some may suffer from urinary frequency and irritable bowel syndrome.
- A stressed person may visit the doctor for numerous physical complaints and suffer from emotional disorders such as anxiety, depression, phobias, cognitive disorders, memory problems, and sleep disorders.

Benefits of prayer

An Ohio study[12] examined the effects of prayer on well-being. Of the 560 respondents, 95 percent classified themselves as religious people; 54 percent were Protestants and 25 percent Catholics. Four types of prayer were identified:

1 Petitionary prayer: asking for material things people may need.
2 Ritual prayer: reading the book of prayers.
3 Meditative prayer: 'feeling', or being, in His presence.
4 Colloquial prayer: talking as to a friend and asking God for guidance in making decisions.

Of all these types of prayer, this study revealed that colloquial prayer correlates best with happiness and religious satisfaction, whereas ritual prayer was associated with a negative effect, producing feelings all the more sad, lonely, tense, and fearful. Talking to God as to a friend, telling Him all our joys and sorrows, can bring happiness, healing, and religious satisfaction. So important is the role of prayer in healing that Dr Larry Dossey said, 'I decided that not to employ prayer with my patients was the equivalent of withholding a potent drug or surgical procedure.'[13]

Many people have tried to solve their problems through yoga, secular meditation, or some similar internalised programme of self-empowerment; however, these methods do not have the same effectiveness. In many cases they are techniques of self-hypnosis.

Spiritual and moral values

Most civilisations are founded on a set of beliefs and moral values that lead to an orderly society. Throughout the centuries, belief in spiritual values has been a strong motivator to treat others well and to develop peaceful human relationships. History demonstrates that faithless and amoral societies become so corrupt that they cannot survive. Belief is fundamental to science as well as to religion. Just as faith in a scientific principle is verified, faith in God is validated when tests show that its application leads to correct conclusions and brings satisfying results. Studies indicate that those with regular spiritual practices who meet with a faith community live longer, live better, and are far less likely to have a stroke or heart attack. Faith can provide strength to overcome stress and destructive habits. Belief can give you peace of mind and enable you to reach your full potential through positive choices. Celebrate belief – it is the foundation of life!

Peace of mind

The Bible says, 'You will keep him in perfect peace, Whose mind is stayed on You, Because he trusts in You.' (Isaiah 26:3, NKJV.) When we have a close relationship with God, we experience peace of mind.

This does not mean that those who believe in God and trust Him implicitly will be free from problems. 'Trouble and turmoil may surround us, yet we enjoy a calmness and peace of mind of which the world knows nothing.

This inward peace is reflected in a . . . vigorous, glowing experience that stimulates all with whom we come in contact. The peace of the Christian depends not upon peaceful conditions in the world about him but upon the indwelling of the Spirit of God.'[14]

As nineteenth-century evangelist Dwight L. Moody is quoted by many as saying:

> 'Trust in yourself, and you are doomed to disappointment.
> 'Trust in your friends, and they will die and leave you.
> 'Trust in money, and you may have it taken from you.
> 'Trust in reputation, and some slanderous tongue may blast it.
> 'But trust in God, and you will never be confounded in time or eternity.'

Trusting in a loving, powerful God provides us with the ability to enjoy a healthful lifestyle. Belief and faith in God enables Him to fill our lives with abundant peace and joy.

---

[1] J. S. Levin, H. Y. Vanderpool, 'Is frequent religious attendance really conducive to better health? Toward an epidemiology of religion', *Social Science and Medicine*, 1987, 24 (7), pp. 589-600

[2] J. D. Kark, et al., *American Journal of Public Health*, 1996, 86 (3), pp. 341-346

[3] J. S. Levin, L. M. Chatters, R. J. Taylor, 'Religious effects on health status and life satisfaction among black Americans', *The Journals of Gerontology, Series B: Psychological Sciences and Social Sciences*, 1995, May, 50 (3), pp. 154-163

[4] C. G. Ellison, 'Race, Religious Involvement and Depressive Symptomatology in a South Eastern US Community', *Social Science and Medicine*, 1995, 40 (11), pp. 1,561-1,572

[5] V. J. Shoenbach, et al., 'Social Ties and Mortality In Evans County, GA', *American Journal of Epidemiology*, 1986, 123, pp. 577-591

[6] C. G. Ellison, 'Religious involvement and subjective well-being', *Journal of Health and Social Behaviour*, 1991, Mar, 32 (1), pp. 80-99

[7] J. W. Dwyer, L. L. Clarke, M. K. Miller, 'The effect of religious concentration and affiliation on county cancer mortality rates', *Journal of Health and Social Behaviour*, 1990, Jun, 31 (2), pp. 185-202

[8] H. G. Koenig, *The Healing Power of Healing Faith*, p. 72, 1999, quoting P. H. Hardesty and K. M. Kirby; 'Relation Between Family Religiousness and Drug Use Within Adolescent Peer Groups', *Journal of Social Behaviour and Personality*, 10 (1), 1995, pp. 42-30

[9] Amoatin and S. J. Bahr, 'Religion, Family and Adolescent Drug Use', *Social Perspectives*, 29 (1), 1986, pp. 53-76

[10] H. G. Koenig, *The Healing Power of Faith* (Simon & Schuster: April, 1999), p. 177

[11] J. Marks, 'A Time Out', *US News & World Report*, 11 December, 1995, pp. 85-97

[12] *Journal of Psychology and Theology*, 1991, 19 (1), pp. 71-83

[13] L. Dossey, *Healing Words: The Power of Prayer and the Practice of Medicine* (New York: HarperCollins Publishers, 1993), p. 18

[14] *The SDA Bible Commentary*, vol. 4 (Hagerstown, Md., Review and Herald Publishing Association, 1966), p. 203

Index

A
Abortion 137
Acid rain 85
Adenoids 9
Adrenaline 41, 46, 145, 151
Aerobics 6, 109
Ageing process 77, 109, 126
AIDS/HIV, African crisis 111
Alcohol 4, 5, 6, 15, 27, 33-35, 37, 43, 64, 96, 111, 113, 116, 121, 122, 124, 125, 132, 135-140
   acute/chronic effects 136-138
   cause & effect table 138
   clinical help available 140
   dependency recovery 139-140
   effects on body 136-137
   effects on sex life 137
   what is it? 135
Alcoholic gastritis 136
Allergen identification 143
Allergens, airborne 142
   common 142
Allergic responses 142
Allergies 141-147
Ammonia, from animal waste 85
Anaemia, and alcohol 136
Angina 31, 37, 38
Angiogram 30, 37
Angioplasty 36
Animal husbandry 85
   products 84
   slaughter 84
Antibodies 9, 10, 14, 15, 141, 142
Anti-cancer drugs 119
Antigen 141, 144, 145
Antihistamines 145
Antioxidants 75, 84, 117, 120
Arteries, blocked 36
Arthritis 6, 38, 65, 83, 91, 146
Attitude 19, 27, 51, 53, 114, 121

B
Bad eating habits, for teeth 69
Bee stings 142
Bible, source of peace 53, 150, 153
Blood pressure 20, 25, 27, 29, 31, 33, 35, 74, 78, 88, 109, 125
   vessels 14, 25, 47, 109, 129, 136, 151
Boils 9, 25
Bowel cancer 73, 84, 87
Bran 72, 87, 128
Breast cancer 113, 116, 121
Breastfed babies 15
Burnout 42
Bypass surgery 36, 54

C
Caffeine 6, 35, 37, 64, 96, 128, 129
Calcium 31, 56, 77
Calories 18, 26, 27, 33, 37, 38, 54, 55, 56, 66, 67, 68, 69, 70, 87, 88, 94, 95, 96, 100, 113, 117, 120, 132, 135
Cancer 110-121, 132, 136
   and diet 117
   cell DNA damage 114
   commonest types 119
   general sites of, table 119
   in Africa 111
   of breast 113, 116, 121
   reducing risk 120-121
   treatment of 119
Carbohydrates 16, 48, 68, 69, 70, 76, 80, 94, 132
Cardiovascular disease 4, 28, 29, 30, 31, 33, 34, 35, 37, 81, 82, 83, 84
Cave dweller's diet 80
Cheerfulness 15, 138
Cheeses, soft 83
Children's teeth 69
Cholesterol 25, 27, 29, 30, 31, 32, 33, 37, 38, 61, 67, 71, 84, 87, 99, 125
Christians 46
Chronic fatigue syndrome 42
Circulation 10, 14, 25, 102, 103, 112, 127, 129, 136, 142
Cold mitten friction 47
Constipation 56, 73, 84, 87, 124
Cooking to conserve vitamins/minerals 58
Coronary arteries 30, 31, 32, 36
Coronary artery disease 25, 31, 32, 34, 35, 91
Cowpox 10
Creator's handiwork 7

D
Dairy produce 77, 84, 88, 116, 118, 147
Defence system, of body 7, 8, 14, 113
Depression 15, 42, 149, 151, 152
Dermatitis 142, 143
Diabetes 16-27
Diverticulitis 83, 84, 87
Divine power 7, 15, 35
Drugs, abuse and use of 111, 119, 122, 123, 124, 125, 129, 142, 144, 145

E
Ears, defence system of 8
Eating, healthily 14, 26, 29, 35, 54-100
   we are what we eat 64-79
E-cigarettes 128
Eczema 65, 142, 143, 146
Eggs, as food 32, 66, 75, 76, 83, 84, 88, 142
Empty calories 27, 69, 70, 88, 96, 100, 113, 132, 135
Endorphins 15
E-numbers 79
Environmental issues 85
Exercise 4, 6, 14, 19, 27, 34, 46, 93, 97, 101-109, 112, 129, 130, 132, 134, 147
   cycling for 105
   for mobility 103-104
   programme for 6, 19, 97, 100, 105, 106, 134
   safe stretches 106-108
   what it can do for you 109
Eyes, defence system of 8

F
Faith, in God 152, 153
Fasting 56, 97
Fibre, importance in diet 33, 73, 87
Food allergens, common 142
   poisoning 83
Food-borne infections 83
Foot-bath, hot, uses for 47
Free radicals 75, 84

G
Gardening, as exercise 34, 46
German measles 12
God, relationship with 153
Good book, a stress buster 45
Greenhouse effect 85

H
Habits, and nervous system 126-131
Hans Selye, stress research pioneer 43
Hay fever 142, 144, 146
Healthy eating 14, 26, 29, 35, 54-100
Heart attacks 6, 20, 22, 29, 34, 35, 38, 42, 74, 81
Heart disease, and stress 29, 33, 35, 37, 41, 42
   reversing the harm done 37
Heart, how it works 30
   needs a workout too 105
Heart Foundation guidelines 37
Hobbies, importance of 47
Holidays, importance of 44
Hormones 14, 46, 66, 116, 151
House dust mites 143
Hydrotherapy 47
Hypersensitivity, to substances 141, 145
Hypertension, chronic 42
Hyposensitisation 144

I
Ideal diet 65
Immune system 7, 9, 10, 13, 14, 15, 74, 78, 87, 112, 113, 114, 116, 121, 132, 146
   in children 11-13
Immunisation 10-14, 146
Iron, in diet 77, 79

J
Jenner, Dr E. (smallpox vaccine) 10
Junk food 20, 27, 70, 100, 120

K
Keeping fit 101-109

L
Laws, of activity and rest 6
  of health 4-7, 65
  of heredity 5
  of mind and spirit 7, 15
  of nutrition 6
  of poisons, abstinence from 6
Lifestyle, for heart disease 28, 29, 37, 38
Lifestyle Heart Trial 37
Liver, cancer of 111
Longevity in Georgians, Hunza and Vilcabamba 82
Longevity Research Institute 37
Lungs, defence system of 8
Lymphatic system 9
Lymphocytes 9, 10

M
Magnesium 78
Malnutrition and obesity 20, 91
Measles 9, 10, 12
Meat eaters, at risk 67, 83
Meat-free diet 90
Meat, not necessary for health 67, 68
Meat substitutes 89
Meningitis 12
Methane 85
Micro-organisms 115
Milk sensitivity 86, 146
Minerals 14, 58, 69, 70, 74-78, 87, 94, 117, 121, 129
MMR vaccine 12
Mobility exercises 103-104
Mouth, defence system of 8
Mumps 12

N
Negative emotions 113, 151
Nervous exhaustion 48
Nettle rash (urticaria) 142, 146
Neutrophils 9
Nicotine 15, 34, 125, 127, 128
  eliminating 127-128
Nose, defence system of 8
Number-one killer, coronary heart disease 28, 41

O
Obesity, definition 21, 91
  diseases of 19, 24, 65, 91, 113, 120
Oesophagus, cancer of 113, 116
Oils 57, 70-73, 75, 76, 88
Olive oil, safest 62, 72, 88, 98
Osteoporosis 83
Outside help, when stopping smoking 133
Overweight children 19, 24

P
Passive immunity, in babies 15
Pastimes, importance of 47
Peace and quiet, need for 48
Pertussis (whooping cough) 11
Phosphorus 77, 78
Phytochemicals 14, 15, 72, 73, 75, 81, 86, 87, 94, 117, 120
Plant food diet, in Bible 65, 86, 92
Plant foods 14, 15, 33, 37, 57, 65, 66, 68, 70, 72, 73, 74, 77, 80-90
Poisoning, food 83
Poisons, avoidance of 6, 64, 112
  in tobacco 34
Polio 10, 11
Pollen count 143
Poor nutrition, in every society 65
Posture 106
Potassium 77, 78
Prayer 15, 65, 123, 133, 152
Preserving the environment 85
Processed foods 72, 78, 120
Prostate cancer 115, 117
Protein, three myths 67-68
  plant protein superior 67

R
Red wine 34-35
Refined food 14, 24, 54, 73, 74, 78, 88, 94, 98, 113, 118
Relaxation techniques 49-50
Release from Tension, book 53
Rest, regular hours for 14, 45
Rhythmic breathing 52
Rubella (German measles) 12

S
Salmonella 83
Saturated fats 71, 72, 84
Seventh-day Adventists 38
Short breaks 44
Skin, defence system of 8, 9, 112
Smallpox 10
Smoking 126-134
Sneezing, wheezing and itches 141-143, 147
Sodium 77, 78
Soft cheeses 83
Source of peace, the Bible 35, 38, 53, 150, 153
Soya milk 59, 63, 77, 86, 99
Spinal cord 77, 137
Spiritual values 152
Starvation mode 55, 56, 94
Stiff neck, exercise for 49-51
Stomach, defence system of 8
  tension 52
Stress 39-53
  effects on back 42
  research, Hans Selye 43
  seekers and copers 41, 42
  signs of 42
Stressors 40
Stretching exercises 106-108
Success as a quitter 126-128, 132, 133
Sugar, consumption of 18, 64, 68, 69
  for instant energy 68
  simple 69
Sunlight, very important 38, 76, 116

T
Taste buds, educating them 86
Tetanus 10, 11
Tobacco 5, 6, 27, 34, 113, 121, 126, 128
  and cancer 113, 120
Tonsils 9
Total abstinence, from alcohol 6, 27
Trace minerals 78
Tranquillisers 15, 122, 123
Trust, in divine power 7, 15, 35, 53, 134, 149, 153

U
Unrefined cereals 37, 48, 57, 89, 99
Unsaturated fats 33, 71, 72

V
Vaccinations 10-13
Valium 122
Varicose veins 65, 91
Variety, the spice of life 14, 37, 57, 58, 68, 79, 80, 88, 89, 90, 99, 112, 118, 120, 121, 146
Vegetable oils 71-73, 88
Vegetarian diet 68, 77, 81-91
Vitamins 75, 76, 87, 94, 121, 129
  B-complex 48, 76, 129
  B12 77

W
Walking, as exercise 34, 93, 98, 105
Warm baths 14, 47
Water, cold, activates immune system 14
  therapy 47
  vital to health 38, 74, 118
Weight control
  best foods for 70, 84, 94-97, 132
  cravings 94, 99
  fasting 56, 97
  practical suggestions 97
  the 'right' weight 92, 93
  when stopping smoking 131, 132
  whole plant food diet 61, 78, 87, 96, 98
Weimar Institute 30, 37
Western diet 5, 18, 24, 94, 117
  lifestyle 18, 24, 28, 64, 83, 91, 111
White blood cells 8, 9, 14, 69, 112, 136
  cell count 14
Whole foods 57, 86, 88
Wholesome food 6
Wholewheat bread 48, 60, 69, 70, 87-90, 94, 98
Whooping cough (pertussis) 11
Workout, heart needs one too 105
Would-be vegetarians 89

155

Juicing for Life

Beverley Ramages has become a regular fresh juice and smoothie maker, and this publication showcases over a hundred of her favourite recipes.

Along with these healthy, easy-to-make and tasty recipes, there is useful information on:
- Selecting the right equipment to get started,
- The values and benefits of the ingredients, and
- The health benefits of each recipe.

All of which will be useful as you begin to develop drinks for your own requirements – for example:
- Weight loss or gain,
- Energy boosting,
- Detoxing, or
- Ensuring that your family get their five-a-day.

The Stanborough Press Ltd

Understanding Nutrition

Dr Clemency Mitchell has had 30 years in general medical practice, even longer teaching college students health principles, running health, nutrition and cookery courses.

'My years in general practice taught me that a change in diet and lifestyle would be by far the best prescription for most chronic health problems,' writes Dr Mitchell.

'Nowadays we are bombarded with information about health, including numerous nutritional theories that often seem to change from day to day.'

She continues, 'The principles underlying this book are not based on such shifting sand but on the age-old principles of the Bible, in particular the story of Creation in the book of Genesis where we learn that the Creator designed a plant-food diet and an active lifestyle with a weekly rest day for the human race.'

She concludes, 'Medical and nutritional science, common sense and experience both in the kitchen and the consulting room confirm that these principles still hold the secrets of good health.'

The Stanborough Press Ltd

Eating for Life

Eating for Life

Clemency Mitchell
Additional contributors: Lucinda Annan, Agnes David, Angeline Francis, Huldah Ogwel, and Thelma Soremekun

Eating healthily needn't be boring – or expensive! This book brings practical vegan cooking and baking to life. It is jam-packed with mouth-watering recipes and food-preparation tips for every occasion, from breakfast to supper and from starters to desserts.

You couldn't wish for a more helpful book when it comes to healthy food preparation. Most of the ingredients are readily available, and every one of these recipes is free of animal products – no meat or dairy produce here! What's more, the author places great emphasis on using whole foods, making this book less about what good cooking doesn't contain, and more about what it does – namely, wholesome, nutritious, tasty goodness, just the way it was intended to be.

The Stanborough Press Ltd